AGENCY AND ORGANIZATION

AGENCY AND ORGANIZATION

Towards an organizational theory of society

Göran Ahrne

SAGE Publications
London · Newbury Park · New Delhi

SAGE Publications Ltd
6 Bonhill Street
London EC2A 4PU

SAGE Publications Inc
2455 Teller Road
Newbury Park, California 91320

SAGE Publications India Pvt Ltd
32, M-Block Market
Greater Kailash – I
New Delhi 110 048

British Library Cataloguing in Publication data

Ahrne, Göran
    Agency and organization: towards an
    organizational theory of society.
    1. Society. Theories
    I. Title
    301.01

    ISBN 0-8039-8292-5
    ISBN 0-8039-8293-3 pbk

Library of Congress catalog card number 90-62093

Typeset by AKM Associates (UK) Ltd, Southall
Printed in Great Britain by Dotesios Printer Ltd,
Trowbridge, Wiltshire

Contents

Acknowledgements

The ideas presented in this book have developed not least through stimulating and candid discussions with colleagues and friends. The theory group at the biennial meeting of the Scandinavian Sociological Association in August 1989, the group for economic sociology at the annual meeting of the Swedish Sociological Association in February 1990 and seminars at the department of sociology in Uppsala and at the Stockholm School of Economics have been particularly encouraging.

Special thanks are due to: Ulla Bergryd, Thomas Brante, Thomas Coniavitis, Mats Franzén, Roine Johansson, Håkon Leiulfsrud, Per-Anders Lindén, Kerstin Sahlin-Andersson, Yohanan Stryjan, Richard Swedberg, Michael Tåhlin, Lars Udéhn, and Mats Wiman.

Finally, I would like to thank my wife, Marianne Ahrne, for her keen support and excellent suggestions. Her careful reading of the manuscript has been invaluable to my work.

1
Social Systems, Social Structures, Social Landscapes

The world and everyday life

The stock market never closes. Every minute the ups and downs of rates are cabled out over the world. The sky is full of satellites continually sending news, the latest rock music and old movies all over the world. In your living-room you can follow in full detail hour by hour the unfolding of a hijacking drama in an airport of some unknown city, but you do not know what your next-door neighbour is doing. The time schedule of the 1988 Olympic Games in South Korea was arranged to suit the convenience of TV viewers in the United States, because the TV rights were sold to an American broadcasting corporation.

The development of modern communications has made it easier for big business to transmit information, money and goods around the earth. For the ordinary TV viewer the discovery of the world in the living-room is a strange experience of involvement and detachment at the same time. You are brought nearer to what appears to be the centre of events but this only heightens your feeling of powerlessness. Your position as an onlooker is even more pronounced. With your remote control you can choose among a number of TV channels but you have no way of interfering with what is going on. The ratio between what you know and watch on the one hand and what you are actually able to do runs higher every day.

The amount of information that is spread around has increased many times over the last decades, but by no means everybody benefits from this growth. If there has been a revolution in the means of information, it has not involved the masses of the people; it has literally been a revolution from above – from the sky. Most information is means-specific; it is of real interest only to those who have the means to use it. If you are deprived of these means, the increasing flood of information becomes more or less meaningless. Information in a general sense is as much a means of control as a means of liberation, if not more so.

In all parts of the world people are moving from the country to big cities where they will have to travel long distances between their home and their place of work, provided they have one. Unemployment, war and starvation drive people away from their families and kin. It is a common experience for rich and poor in today's world that their everyday life is becoming disconnected. It is not a totally new phenomenon, but from being a trend it has now become a dominant feature of social life. On a macro-level the world is becoming increasingly intertwined, while the everyday life of ordinary people becomes more and more disintegrated.

Ever larger amounts of food and the other primary commodities that people need for survival are transported over long distances within or between countries: grains, vegetables, oil are among these. The various parts of your car, television set, or refrigerator are manufactured in many countries. This forms a long chain of interdependence between human activities transmitted through the artefacts of labour. It is not a dependence on real people whom you can see and talk to. The collective character of human life is hidden in technological connections; it is a sequential dependence: a dependence on abstract messages and symbols – computerized messages, money orders, telecommunications of various kinds. Even talking to somebody on the telephone is an abstract relation. It is not an immediate communication between living human beings. Different components of your everyday world are connected with remote parts of the earth. The geographical world is becoming entangled in a network of competing centres of power with global possibilities of control, while the everyday world of ordinary people is slipping apart.

The world-scale of trade, communications, travel, crime, sports, advertising, creates an intertwinement at the macro-level but this is not to say that the world is becoming one. There is not one world system. There is a growing overlap of the social phenomena we usually regard as systems, structures, societies or organizations. Social life is becoming denser but it is not unified.

There is a mingling of social forms on a world-scale. Power centres have acquired longer tentacles that interfere in local markets, politics and culture. New means of communication and organization stretch into foreign everyday worlds where they have no meaning except as seekers of control.

The world of the New Theoretical Movement

Social theory is not a world of its own. It should have some relationship with the social world as we know it. The aim of the preceding pages has been to give a hint of such a connection to prepare for a critical discussion of what has been called the New Theoretical Movement within the social sciences.

The founding of this movement coincides with the publication of the 1988 edition of the *Handbook of Sociology*, in which Jeffrey Alexander wrote an insightful article on the development of sociological theorizing during the last ten years. This article bears the title 'The New Theoretical Movement'. As with so many movements its raison d'être is the more or less sudden change of a phenomenon within its realm. 'Sociological theory is at a turning point' (1988a: 77). But what is the purpose of this new movement? Is it only to put sociological theory right again?

Generally speaking, it seems to be a nice, gentle movement. It is tolerant towards deviations and among its supporters 'there remain fundamental disagreements'. There is, however, a common platform for its activity: the battle-cry is 'neither micro nor macro theory is satisfactory'. And its programme is formulated thus: 'Action and structure must now be intertwined' (1988a: 77).

Its politics are very peaceful, though. It does not build any barricades and its programme is far from revolutionary. In fact, its ideology is firmly rooted in the revisionist tradition. 'It is by studying revisionism within the micro and macro traditions that the new theoretical movement in sociology can be revealed' (Alexander, 1988a: 89).

Actually, one wonders whether this movement has any enemies at all. It seems that all its potential adversaries have destroyed themselves. In a way the movement operates in a waste land. Its aim is to construct, not to conquer. The situation is well described in the words of Theda Skocpol: 'Ours is an era when no existing macrosociological theory seems adequate, yet when the need for valid knowledge of social structures and transformations has never been greater' (1984: 385). This seemingly unchallenged position of the movement may explain its rather bloodless and quiet appearance. There is a lack of vigour in the movement, it has a flavour of avant-garde and self-sufficiency at the same time. Although one has to agree with its general goals and aims one also has to fear the transformation of the movement into a mutual admiration society. There is a risk that the connection between micro- and macrotheory will have very little to do with relations between the world and the everyday lives of ordinary people.

In his article in the *Handbook of Sociology* Alexander describes the debate concerning micro and macro or action and structure in sociology as a pendulum (1988a: 83). Talcott Parsons attempted to bridge this gap, but failed. All the critics of Parsons have virtually had to choose sides, either micro or macro. According to Alexander, this split has been typical of the variations of sociological theory during the sixties and seventies.

Today, however, Alexander argues, the anti-Parsonian movement is over, for the simple reason that it won (1987: 375). Even though the anti-Parsonians were the winners, they have been less successful in establishing an alternative theoretical construction. At least that is the standpoint of the various representatives of the New Theoretical Movement. Alexander is optimistic: 'This new generation of theorists have made efforts to close the dialectic, to provide a "third way" that takes the best of each side' (1987: 376).

In another article Alexander, together with Bernhard Giesen, takes a long view of the issue of micro and macro in social theory. Alexander and Giesen maintain that the micro-macro dichotomy should be understood as an analytic distinction to be found in several schools of thought and crossing paradigmatic boundaries (1988: 257). It has a far-reaching philosophical background and it can be traced in all the sociological classics. Max Weber was one of the first to attempt a synthetic formulation. Since then the pendulum has been swinging and once again it is time for a new effort to bind the two poles together.

Alexander and Giesen distinguish five main ways to

analyse the relationship between the micro- and the macro-level. Either rational or interpretative individuals create society through contingent acts of freedom. Socialized individuals may either recreate society through contingent acts of freedom or reproduce society by translating the existing social environment in the micro-realm. Finally, rational and purposeful individuals may acquiesce in society because they are forced to by external, social control (1988: 270). The variations in these perspectives thus stem from assumptions about individual behaviour, as well as from the nature of social reality. Combinations of these perspectives can appear within the work of any one theorist.

Who then are the members of the new movement? In his article 'Sociological theory today' (1988a), Alexander mentions one important starting point for this whole tendency, namely, the publication in 1981 of the anthology *Advances in Social Theory and Methodology: Toward an Integration of Micro- and Macro-sociologies*, edited by Karen Knorr-Cetina and Aaron Cicourel. In this volume, which has 16 contributors, some of the better-known figures of the movement are represented, among them Jürgen Habermas, Anthony Giddens and Randall Collins. These three are also especially mentioned by Alexander. Another anthology should also be regarded as belonging to the canonical texts: the volume *The Micro–Macro Link* which was edited by, among others, Alexander and Giesen. It appeared in 1987 but its articles go back to a conference held in 1984. (For a more comprehensive survey of representative works, see Alexander, 1988a: 89–93.)

After this presentation of the new theoretical agenda I think it will be useful to take a closer look at two of its best-known contributions, namely, some later works of Habermas and Giddens, before going into a more general critical discussion of its accomplishments so far. Now, it is far from certain that Habermas or Giddens would like to be seen as representatives of a new theoretical movement. In fact, Giddens has criticized the idea of formulating theories in terms of micro and macro, since 'an unhappy division of labour tends to come into being between them' (1984: 139). In lumping together various theoretical efforts in terms of micro/ macro, action/structure or individual/society into one theoretical project, one runs the risk of losing important distinctions between them. Still, I think these various approaches to social theory have so many common aspects that it is justifiable to treat them as belonging to the same broad trend of theorizing; they also display some common shortcomings.

System and lifeworld

With his theory of communicative action in relation to the complementary concepts of system and lifeworld Habermas seeks to address the paradoxes of the process of rationalizing modern social life (1985: 419). In his discussion he starts from a critique of Weber and the application of Weber's notion of rationalization that was attempted by certain Marxist writers, notably Georg Lukács, Max Horkheimer and Theodor Adorno. According to Habermas, their analysis of the process of rationalization led them into a blind alley, since 'the rationalization of society has constantly been thought of as a reification of consciousness' (1984: 399). In their work Horkheimer and Adorno have not been able to separate system rationality on the one hand and, on the other, the rationality of action. Thus, they have confused the process of the structuration of the lifeworld with the evolution of the steering capacity of differentiated social systems. The world of Critical Theory has been a one-dimensional world. And Habermas asserts that this was the reason why 'they could locate the spontaneity that was not yet in the grips of the

reifying force of systemic rationalization only in irrational powers' (1987: 333). For Habermas the lack of
connection between a lifeworld perspective and a system
perspective is of importance because it makes it possible
to analyse the rationalization of the lifeworld as a
phenomenon distinct from the rationalization of the
system. These two processes may or may not coincide
and the way they are linked is of crucial importance to
understanding the quality of modern life and the nature
of social conflicts today. It is, moreover, in this inter-
section between system and lifeworld that the theory of
communicative action has a role to play.

The relationship between system and lifeworld is
delicate and Habermas sees the possible complexity in
each lifeworld as limited (1985: 214). When the connection between system and lifeworld is distorted,
Habermas considers this to be a 'colonization' of the
lifeworld. This colonization, however, seems not to be
normal even in modern social life. The normal exchange
between system and lifeworld is called 'mediatization'
and is conducted via the two principal media, money and
power.

In my discussion of Habermas I shall not touch upon
the theory of communicative action at all, but shall
concentrate on how Habermas deals with and concep-
tualizes the system. The subtitle of the second volume of
The Theory of Communicative Action is 'To the Critique of
Functionalist Reason'. Still, it is astonishing to note how
much Habermas is influenced by Parsons in his terminology, as well as in his way of looking at the social
system. Distinguishing him from Parsons, however, is
the importance of a historical approach to the gradual
decoupling of a social system from the lifeworld; how
the distance between the two poles of social life has
increased and how their integration has become more
and more complicated (1987: 155).

In describing the separation of a system from the

lifeworld, Habermas distinguishes three periods of increasing system complexity. In tribal societies the differentiation occurs through systems of kinship, rules of marriage and the formation of prestige. The differentiation takes place in close contact with the routines of daily life; its mechanisms have not yet become detached from 'institutions effective for social integration' (1987: 163)

On the second level of system differentiation the mechanisms of state power free themselves from the kinship structures (1987: 165). A politically stratified class society emerges. In later phases of this development the state becomes specialized into administrative, military and legal institutions.

The third level of system differentiation comes into being with the rise of the capitalist economic system. What is most important to Habermas in the advent of capitalism is the dominance of a new medium of exchange, namely, money. He calls it a new steering medium. Money is a steering medium of great capacity and far-reaching importance. Habermas emphasizes that it is only after becoming 'an intersystemic medium of interchange' that it has had 'structure-forming effects' (1987: 171).

In developing this third level of system differentiation, the social system has finally relieved itself of 'the horizon of the lifeworld'. Habermas expresses this as a challenge to the assimilative powers of the lifeworld; its meaning contexts are depleted. 'In a differentiated social system the lifeworld seems to shrink to a subsystem' (1987: 173).

For the purpose of analysing these increasing tensions between system and lifeworld, Habermas introduces a typology of forms of understanding. Different system levels demand different forms of understanding. The modern form of understanding is fragile; it is transparent, making the systemic suppression of social integration visible, and the whole 'symbolic reproduction of the lifeworld is at stake' (1987: 196). At this point the mediatization of the lifeworld may turn into a colonization. For Habermas the conflict potential in modern political life will be situated 'along the seams between system and lifeworld' (1987: 395). But when it comes to the transformation of mediatization into colonization, he only gives general hints on how to perceive this process.

We have followed the growth and gradual emancipation of a social system from the lifeworld, which leaves an increased complexity behind. But what has become of this system? In fact, Habermas has surprisingly little to say about the system itself. The system is made up of two subsystems, namely, capitalism and the apparatus of the modern state. They have been differentiated from the lifeworld through the media of money and power (1987: 318). More concretely, the exchange between the two subsystems and the lifeworld takes the form of, for instance, labour power, goods and services, taxes, political decisions and mass loyalty (1987: 320). The media utilized for these exchanges are either money or power. Typically, the exchange between the subsystem of capitalism and the lifeworld occurs via money, whereas the exchange between the state and the lifeworld is mediated via power relations. Money is also used in the exchange between the lifeworld and the state, however.

It seems as if Habermas is interested merely in what takes place between the system and the lifeworld. In his thick book he does not say one word about the relationship between the two subsystems, capitalism and the state, or how they are made into a system. This is a serious lacuna in his theory construction. In a later article Habermas merely establishes the fact that the market oriented economy and the state with its monopoly of violence are intertwined (1985: 411). One aspect of the systemness of the two subsystems is Habermas' opinion that class conflicts in modern social life have become institutionalized and 'shifted out of the life-world into the system' (1987: 348). This might have been an argument in favour of the making of a system, but Habermas does not pursue this thought and the reader is left in ignorance of what mechanisms and processes make the two distinct subsystems into a system. One is left in doubt about whether these two subsystems are the only subsystems, about the range of the system, the nature of its boundaries, and its relations to other systems or subsystems. Are money and power thought of as the only media? It also seems that these 'media' are very different in kind, which makes their unification into one system problematic. Money refers to a concrete object that has a special institutionalized role in social life, whereas power is an abstract concept that may have many kinds of incarnations in human relations.

I would argue that the vagueness of Habermas' idea of the system makes his approach towards the problems of the exchange between system and lifeworld un-necessarily abstract, thereby giving room for misunder-standings about the colonization of the lifeworld. In investigating events in the lifeworld one has to focus on the relations of individuals with particular organizations such as schools, supermarkets or factories. People do not have any direct connections with systems or subsystems.

System, structure and structuration

There is apparently a high level of tolerance and freedom of opinion within the New Theoretical Move-ment. Whereas Habermas, and also Alexander, hold the sociology of Talcott Parsons in high esteem (although Habermas has criticized functionalist reason), Anthony Giddens has proclaimed his theory of structuration a non-functionalist manifesto (1979: 7). In his later book

The Constitution of Society, Giddens underlines this stand-point and declares that a 'radical break has to be made with Parsonian theorems' (1984: xxxvi). In doing this, he explicitly criticizes Habermas and Alexander, among others, for being too respectful towards the legacy of Talcott Parsons.

However, even Giddens takes up the thread from functionalist thinking when he stresses the importance of understanding the unintended consequences of social behaviour. He contrasts functionalist social thinking with action theories of behaviour, 'which have simply ignored unintended consequences'. He thus gives credit to the functionalists for highlighting the significance of unintended consequences of behaviour in analysing the reproduction of social systems. Giddens, however, has an altogether different way of dealing with such processes.

For Giddens action theory is not enough, but the notion of system is problematic. He is trying to overcome both the imperialism of the subject in inter-pretative sociologies and the imperialism of the social object in functionalism and structuralism. According to his theory of structuration neither individual actors nor social totalities are the principal objects, 'but the social practices ordered across space and time' (1984: 2).

In his approach to action Giddens takes a largely phenomenological stance, with influences from Alfred Schutz but also from psychoanalytic theory. Some key concepts in his description of action are: the durée, ability to go on, routinization, practical and discursive consciousness. The typical activities of everyday life are conducted by reflexive monitoring of action (1984: 5). The idea of practical consciousness seems to imply that actions are neither altogether unconscious nor fully rational. They are marked by routines and habits. Giddens writes: 'Much of our day-to-day conduct is not directly motivated' (1984: 6). He talks of 'grey areas' of consciousness.

The idea of reflexive monitoring of actions is connected with the importance of unintended consequences. Even if individuals can control their bodies and movements when acting, they can seldom control the effects of these actions to any extent. Things happen that were not intended and sometimes intentions are realized but not by the expected means. 'The unintended consequences are regularly "distributed" as a by-product of regularized behaviour reflexively sustained as such by its participants' (1984: 14). It is pointed out that unintended consequences need not be bad. They are essential, however, in understanding the relations between actions and a social system. This is where the duality of structure comes in, the idea that 'agents and structures are not two independently given sets of phenomena, a dualism, but represent a duality' (1984: 25).

Through the distribution of unintended consequences, human activity also reproduces the social system. Giddens puts this idea nicely in an aphoristic formulation: 'Human history is created by intentional activities but is not an intended project' (1984: 27). One cannot but interpret this as saying that history is a series of unintended consequences, even though Giddens does not state this clearly.

The three core concepts in the structuration theory are structure, system and the duality of structure (1984: 16). To try to grasp the argument of reproduction through unintended consequences, we must now turn to the system and the structure themselves. The important point here is that Giddens distinguishes between a system and a structure. Instead of seeing the whole as a system or a structure, he sees a structure, which patterns human activities, and a system, which is being reproduced. Structure is seen as 'the properties which make it possible for discernibly similar social practices to exist across varying spans of time and space' (1984: 17). The concept of structure refers to the ways in which systems are reproduced. These ways are called 'structural principles' (see also 1984: 185). One aspect of these principles is 'rules' in a general sense. Although allowing that the idea of rules may be problematic, Giddens maintains that rules are important for understanding the working of the structure. Furthermore, rules are regarded as techniques 'applied in the enactment/reproduction of social practices' (1984: 21). In a way structure may be understood as a filter above or in front of the system.

Another aspect of the structure is the existence of institutions, which are the structural mechanisms with 'the greatest time–space extension' (1984: 17). Rules and institutions seem to be highly intertwined, however. On page 22 of *The Constitution of Society* Giddens writes that the most significant rules 'are locked into the reproduction of institutionalized practices'. He also proposes a classification of institutional orders in distinguishing between symbolic orders, political, economic and legal institutions (1984: 31–3).

In his structuration theory Giddens thus suggests several ways of comprehending the idea of a structure that filters and patterns the reproduction of a system. But he has very little to say about how the different aspects of the structure come together, such as the institutional orders: whether they cooperate, compete, overlap, or work independently of each other. In fact, one wonders what holds the structure together, what makes it a structure at all? And what is it actually that is being reproduced?

Giddens defines system(s) thus: 'Reproduced relations between actors or collectivities, organized as regular social practices' (1984: 25). It is a very general description indeed, and seems much like the definition of sociology given in elementary introductions. If the idea of a system in Giddens' theory is so vague and general, the intent in separating structure from system is lost altogether. What is the point in having a concept for something that may be anything, only provided it is being reproduced? Giddens says something about what systems are not. They are not 'clusters of social relations whose boundaries are clearly set off from others' (1984: 165). And they are not to be equated with societies, since there exist what Giddens refers to as 'intersocietal systems' (1984: 184). There are also, according to Giddens, degrees of systemness (1984: xxvi, 165).

The discussion of the concepts of system and society is interesting, however. Societies 'stand out in bas-relief from a background of a range of other systemic relationships in which they are embedded'. The reason they are separated from systems is that they somehow happen to be a 'clustering of institutions across time and space' (1984: 164). Societies seem to be a special form of systems. Still, societies contain systemic relationships and they are at the same time contained in intersocietal systems. Giddens stresses that one merit of the structuration theory is that the closure of societies across space and time is regarded as problematic (1984: 165). I find this an important conclusion in general, but I cannot see that it helps to clarify the concept of system. The boundaries of societies are indeed problematic, but what about the boundaries of systems? Furthermore, what are the relations between systems and structures? Is there one structure to every system or is it possible that systems can share structures, or conversely, that structures stretch over several systems? If it is to be at all possible to use the structuration theory in understanding the real world, one must be able to answer these questions. The efforts that Giddens makes in this direction in his book (see 1984: 184-5) do not give any clues to the substance of the distinction between structure and system. If a system may be part of a society, which in its turn may be part of an intersocietal system, where do the structures and the institutional orders come in?

The arbitrary character of these concepts is further reinforced when combined with the idea of the unintended consequences of actions. Is the unintendedness inscribed in the structural principles? Giddens leaves the notion of unintended consequences behind when he stops discussing individual actions. Instead, he takes up the concept of power. But he never clarifies the contradictory relationship between unintended consequences and power and how they are related to structure and system. He only mentions that structure 'is always both constraining and enabling' (1984: 25, see also 175).

A New Grand Theory?

In my account of the New Theoretical Movement, I have emphasized the similarities between various approaches. Despite important epistemological and ontological differences between them, there is such striking likeness as regards style and form that they may be criticized together. But there are also striking similarities in detail among some of its representatives.

One example of similarity of detail is the action theories of Giddens and Alexander, which in their turn may be traced back to 1967, in Peter Berger and Thomas Luckmann's book, *The Social Construction of Reality*. The common ground for this likeness is of course the phenomenological heritage. When Alexander writes about the typification of actions, he comes very close to what Giddens calls routinization. Alexander writes: 'The most basic rule for acquiring sociological citizenship is no surprise' (1988b: 313). To Giddens it is the ability to go on. Berger and Luckmann describe the origin of habitualization of actions with the words 'There I go again'. For the individual the meaning of actions 'be-comes embedded as routines in his general stock of knowledge' (1967: 53). Habermas also has this phenomenological approach, although he is not as out-spoken as these writers. Some variation of a pheno-menological position, be it ethnomethodology or her-meneutics, to grasp the micro-situation is one common denominator within the movement, however.

Both Habermas and Giddens use the concept of system, although in quite divergent manners. Apart from the system itself, Habermas talks about two subsystems, whereas Giddens has supplemented the system with a patterning structure. However different in their general approaches to some macro-entity, I think there are important problems that Habermas and Giddens have in common. Neither of them has managed to describe the relationship between what they call the system and institutions or organizations. The basic question should be: Are organizations really brought together into a system and, if they are, how does this happen? Another question concerns the boundaries of the system in relation to such phenomena as the capitalist system and the nation-state. Habermas only vaguely assumes that capitalism and the state are intertwined. Giddens regards institutions in general as an aspect of a structure that somehow patterns the system. In fact, neither Habermas nor Giddens gives any evidence of the existence of a system separating itself from other systems. Is it at all necessary that the macro-level is conceived of as a system? If the idea of a system extends onto a world-scale it loses its meaning.

Under the heading 'Terminological Concerns', Alexander, in his book *Action and its Environments*, writes about the twin concepts micro/macro. First he suggests that an 'equation of micro with individual is extremely misleading' (1988b: 302). This seems quite sensible. But then he goes on to state: 'There can be no empirical referents for micro or macro as such.' They are only regarded as 'analytical contrasts' (1988b: 9). The relationship between micro and macro is seen as 'completely relativistic' (1988b: 303). This seems to me to be the big flaw in this kind of reasoning. The idea of a system in the writings of both Habermas and Giddens is problematic just because it does not have any empirical referents. In this way the use of the term 'system' becomes too abstract and very arbitrary. It tries to denote something that presumably holds together, but we do not know why, how, or where.

In an effort to materialize and concretize the idea of a social system, Alexander declares that the social system is the environment for action 'by providing actors with real objects' (1988b: 317). These objects may be automobiles or horses and very often other human beings. To regard the social system as simply an environment for actions seems to be a meaningless use of the concept. Later in the text Alexander also talks about interactive systems at different levels and different sizes (1988b: 328). But my question is: When the macro-system is such a nebulous concept, why not pay a little more attention to the institutional orders instead? Perhaps we would do better not to bother about systems or structures at all.

We know that through modern technology large organizations, at an increasing tempo and over longer distances, are influencing the everyday lives of more and more people all over the world. In this perspective the aim of the New Theoretical Movement, that action and structure must be intertwined, seems somewhat obsolete. Generally speaking, the New Theoretical Movement appears to be remarkably unaware of what is going on in contemporary social life.

I find the critique that C. Wright Mills delivered against what he called Grand Theory, in his book *The Sociological Imagination* of 1959, very telling, even thirty years later. His criticism was first of all aimed at Parsons and his followers, but it may be applied equally well to the New Theoretical Movement. Mills writes: 'This absence of a firm sense of genuine problems, in turn, makes for the unreality so noticeable in their pages.' Mills argues that the grand theorists deal too much with the relations between concepts instead of considering what they stand for: 'Grand theory is drunk on syntax, blind to semantics' (1970: 42).

It is a lamentable fact that there is a tendency to unnecessary abstraction in social theory. Although much criticism has been levelled against Parsons, some of his most eager critics have ended up in a position that in many respects corresponds to his way and style of theorizing. I have abstained from doing what Mills did, namely, rewrite pages from Parsons in a few sentences. This method could have been applied to several of the texts from the New Theoretical Movement. Mills concluded that many ideas of the grand theorists, in fact, when shortened, were 'more or less standard ones available in many textbooks of sociology' (1970: 38). It is a regrettable fact that the New Theoretical Movement to a large extent has become a New Grand Theory.

The history of what?

If there are no systems to talk about, what then do we have? In his book *Big Structures, Large Processes, Huge Comparisons*, Charles Tilly, one of the leading proponents of historical sociology, distinguishes eight 'Pernicious Postulates' of traditional social theory. The first of these is that 'society' is regarded as a thing apart. Tilly argues that the idea that the social world is divided into distinct societies with more or less autonomous cultures and political lives is a big and devastating mistake (1984: 7–8). It hinders theoretical and empirical analysis. First of all there are practical problems involved when it comes to checking 'the clarity and stability of social boundaries thus produced'. Moreover, the analysis will be unnecessarily restricted when describing 'the coherent structures and processes presumably contained within those boundaries' (1984: 22). One illustration that Tilly gives is the discussion about 'German society'. But Tilly's conclusion is: 'German society, as such, did not exist' (1984: 23).

Immanuel Wallerstein in an article, 'Societal development, or development of the world-system?', has also discussed German society as a problematic concept. He is just as critical as Tilly towards the use of the idea of societies as social entities. He argues that using the concept of society 'reifies and therefore crystallises social phenomena whose real significance lies not in their solidity but precisely in their fluidity and malleability' (1986: 9). According to Giddens, societies were distinguishable because they were a clustering of institutions in a certain time and space. For Tilly and Wallerstein, however, this clustering may not best be understood and analysed as a separate unit, a thing apart. It may rather be understood in connection with other institutions of the same kind. The clustering itself may be occasional and its boundaries arbitrary. The concept of society hides more than it discloses.

Criticism of the idea of societies as social units has most often been delivered by historically oriented sociologists. This may have something to do with the fact that the boundaries of societies in the social sciences have usually been regarded as coinciding with the borders of the nation-states. In a historical perspective the impossibility of this conventional view becomes apparent. A sociologically oriented historian, Fernand Braudel, in his investigation of civilization and capitalism 1400–1800, finds the idea of unitary societies highly problematic. He says that for the historian society is 'not a single container, but several containers and their contents' (1982: 458). Instead of the concept of society, Braudel regards social reality as 'a set of sets' (1982: 459). He describes what has been called feudal society as containing four or five such sets, including the Catholic church, the territorial state, the cities. He maintains that this was 'not one system but several; not one hierarchy but several; not one order but several' (1982: 465).

If we are to take this critique seriously, we now have neither systems nor societies to lean on when analysing the macro-level of social life. Or maybe we can use Braudel's containers. Tilly talks about big structures and large processes. But he adds: 'The analyses should be concrete in having real times, people and places as their referents' (1984: 14). This is quite opposed to Alexander's view of the micro/macro distinction. Big structures and large processes certainly are vague concepts, but Tilly's point is that these processes should not be regarded in isolation from real events.

Michael Mann is another sociologist who has turned towards history and discovered the problems of the concept of society. Perhaps he is the one who has most thoroughly elaborated this critique. On the first page of his book *The Sources of Social Power: Volume 1* he states: 'Societies are not unitary. They are not social systems (closed or open); they are not totalities' (1986: 1). Further on he also explicitly repudiates any use of a distinction between action and structure (1986: 2). For Mann the unique development that took place in Europe during and after the Middle Ages 'was not the result of the dynamism or the contradictions of a preceding social system' (1986: 506). He regards the whole process as a 'gigantic series of coincidences' (1986: 505). The patterning of this development 'contained several disparate power networks whose interaction encouraged social and economic development'. And the origins of the components of the actual structure 'lie in a great diversity of times and places' (1986: 504).

Society is neither a theoretically fruitful concept, nor

an empirically meaningful entity. Instead, Mann conceives of 'societies as multiple overlapping and intersecting power networks' (1986: 2). Instead of systems or societies there are clearly distinguishable networks of power, the interaction of which determines historical development in seemingly unpredictable ways. Mann distinguishes between four such networks of power: ideology, economy, military and state. Apart from these four networks, Mann also acknowledges the existence of a number of unspecified casual sequences, which are 'too complex to be theorized' (1986: 29). The four power networks, though, are distinguishable from 'the messiness of human societies'. But Mann concludes: 'Our theories can only encompass some of their broadest contours' (1986: 30).

I find Mann's approach to a description of a social macro-level quite fruitful and stimulating. The idea of power networks makes sense in a general way and the concepts have a firm robustness in comparison with systems or societies. Still, it is far from clear what kind of distinguishable network of power ideology would be in today's world. And it seems that economy is far too general a term to be very illuminating as one network of power. There are too many kinds of economy and it is indeed a delicate task to try to delineate economic activities from other social activities. Moreover, I think that Mann has given up a little too easily in his efforts to theorize other complex causal sequences. There are other social processes that might have been thought of as networks of power just as well as ideology, such as kinship, gender or culture.

The social landscape

The world we live in is not neatly arranged and laid out. It is not like a seventeenth-century garden, where every corner of a flower bed is part of a formal plan and where every bend of a walk is carefully patterned. Our world has grown from multiple processes of various kinds. Only limited areas are the outcome of conscious planning, and even they may not look today as they were intended. The social world is more like a rough landscape which is the result of long chains of development: a mountain crumbling away, a forest growing, a desert spreading, a motorway under construction. A landscape is the coincidence of several phenomena with different origins and nature and, in fact, with little in common except that they happen to be near each other at a certain point in time.

The metaphor of a landscape is a telling one. A picturesque scene looks perfectly integrated: a few houses, a river with a bridge over it, a meadow, a forest, a mountain, flowers, a horse, some clouds, an old rusty tractor. But this apparent integration is illusory. Basically these objects function independently of each other. There are also interdependencies among them, however. The flowers need soil to grow in, and the house has to stand on firm ground. The bridge is there because of the river. But it is impossible to understand the existence of the house with the help of the other objects in the landscape. The shape of the clouds may depend to some extent on the existence of a mountain, but most of the explanation must be found in climatological processes far away. The construction of the tractor has nothing to do with the horse. The landscape is not a unit. The objects in it do not form an analytical totality. Is it at all possible to explain the whole landscape? One would need to draw together insights from a whole lot of different theories such as architecture, botany, geology, and mechanics in attempting such a grandiose explanation. But most often there is no common taxonomy to make a complete explanation possible.

To return to the park of the baroque era, its apparent integration is, in fact, also illusory. The planned design of the park is superficial. The plan, if at all implemented, will explain very little. The trees, the water, the rocks, the grass, the flowers, the sculptures, all have their own histories and origins. One can cut a tree but it still grows. One can build fountains but only in accordance with the general laws of motion of water. And certainly, if one wants to understand what happens in a park during a longer period of time, the human design does not explain much at all.

What is regarded as a society or a system may be likened to a park. A society can have some overall design, some common characteristics that look integrated. But after some time it will be obvious that this superficial integration is illusory. The important processes at work are of different kinds stretching far beyond the boundaries of what looked like a limited totality. I think that what 'stands out', to use Giddens' expression, and makes certain clusterings of institutions look like societies, is of this kind, a superficial common design which has some importance. But the really significant processes may be hidden if one stresses the superficial unity at the cost of the occasional coincidence of divergent phenomena. That is why I think it advisable to avoid reasoning in terms of systems or societies and instead use the metaphor of social landscapes. A social landscape is a mingling of diverse social processes and phenomena that happen to coincide in a certain place at a certain time.

As mentioned above there are also interactive processes going on in a landscape; ecological processes between the objects of the landscape and its environment, that is, other objects. These are processes not directly related to the inner logics of the present objects. They are processes of another kind. In my scenery these phenomena are, for instance, the exact meandering of the river, the slope of the meadow, the rust on the tractor, the form of the mountain. These are slow processes of erosion, abrasion, bleaching, oxidizing, occurring between objects. These changes depend on the strength of various objects in their relations to the nearest environment. Their strength, however, emanates from their origins and their inner logic. The strength of the river depends on the inflow of water. The strength of the house depends on its construction. At every moment the landscape seems to be in a state of balance. Behind this apparent harmony, however, there are several forces striving with different means to change the landscape. In the social landscape actors struggle to increase their control with their particular power resources. Power is not always visible, but the particular constellations of phenomena in a social landscape may, to a large extent, be comprehended in terms of their relative strength. What constitutes strength and power, however, varies with the situation. In the long run the water will undermine the mountain.

What does a social landscape look like? What components can there be? I am convinced that it is best to be as concrete as possible about this. Landscapes are visible. Even if one cannot see the whole mountain one can see a part of it. I suppose that one common component of a social landscape is the nation-state. There is no need to be abstract about the nation-states of the world. In fact, there are not many of them and one can easily count them. Other common components may be capitalist enterprises. One does not have to be too abstract about them either. And I believe that it is much more fruitful to treat nation-states and capitalist enterprises as separate entities than to mix them into a system and lose degrees of concreteness. The processes between nation-states and capitalist enterprises are more of an external type than of an inner-logic type. Further possible components of a social landscape are interest organizations, families, cultures, languages, blending into various fancy combinations. They will meet and interact in many kinds of constellations. There are no distinct levels in the components that can mingle only with a corresponding level of another component. Nearly all kinds of interaction are possible.

The phenomena that make up a landscape are of both a social and a physical nature (cf. Soja, 1985: 92). Most social phenomena have a material form of one kind or another. They are not only material forms, but these forms are important for explaining power resources and action strategies. Capitalist enterprises may take the form of large process industries or of real estate. Nation-states may be materialized as schools, railways or prisons. Cultures and languages are materialized as books, signs, symbols, paintings. In this respect one can really look at social landscapes. This is in fact one important aspect of social life that is brought out in a geographical approach to social phenomena. It is one of the merits of Foucault's discussions of the changes of power structures. His analysis of modern techniques of power, as materialized in the prison model of the Panopticon, is a very illuminating example of the importance of material form for understanding social processes (1979: 195–228).

In a landscape there are also certain kinds of terrain. The terrain keeps the objects together. The terrain itself can be a mixture of many substances. To know the terrain is extremely important in order to be able to orient oneself in the social landscape. In a reader with the title *Geography Matters*, Doreen Massey writes in her introduction that the social sciences 'continued to function, by and large, as though the world operated, and society existed, on the head of a pin, in a spaceless, geographically undifferentiated world' (1984: 4). Her point is this: 'Spatial distributions and geographical differentiation may be the result of social processes, but they also affect how these processes work' (1984: 4). Massey distinguishes certain aspects of spatiality of importance for analysing the social world such as distance, movement, place (1984: 5). Another aspect is territoriality, which may be a highly efficient method of social classification and power (see Sack, 1986).

Finally, the social landscape is inhabited by people. They give life to the landscape. Without people there would not be any social landscape. It is made up of the artefacts of individual and collective actions. In the social landscape individuals move in and out of organizations distributed across the terrain. Organizations are spatially spread out in different kinds of terrain consisting of manifold social phenomena and physical objects. The interaction between individuals and organizations, as well as the interaction between organizations, must be comprehended in relation to their positions in the terrain, which keep them together.

2

The Organizational Scenery

Paradigms lost

One of the most obvious features of the social landscapes of the modern world is the increasing occurrence
of organizations. Organizations are covering ever larger
areas of the social as well as the geographical space of the
earth. While the rain forests are being devastated, the
organizational networks are spreading and becoming
tighter. Small organizations are integrated into larger
units. A concentration of the organizational flora is
taking place all the time. Old forms of organizing
become obsolete.

To Habermas it looks as if the skyline of the system is
growing higher and higher above the horizon of the
lifeworld. But he does not see any organizations, only
subsystems. For Giddens, too, the growth of organizations is disguised as structures and systems. Neither
Habermas nor Giddens is able to analyse this significant
social development, since they see only the forest and
not the trees. It is impossible to understand why a forest
is growing without looking at the trees.

In order to figure out why the organizational scenery
is growing and how this process affects social life in
general, one has to penetrate the organizational scenery
and examine in more detail what kinds of organization
flourish in different kinds of terrain and how the

interaction between different types of organization is determined by their conditions of growth.

What theoretical tools are there to help us penetrate the organizational scenery? It seems natural to turn to the body of thought and research within the social sciences that comes under the heading 'organization theory'. But organization theory is a rather disorganized field of various theoretical approaches. Organizations have often been regarded as a 'meso-level' between the micro and the macro (cf. Collins, 1988: 251). But if one is sceptical of the idea of levels of social analysis such an approach is not very helpful.

Paul DiMaggio and Walter Powell have made an interesting observation on the paradoxical relationship between macrosocial theories and research on organizations. They have noted that it often seems as if societies are smart while organizations are dumb. They ask: 'How can it be that the confused and contentious bumblers that populate the pages of organizational case studies and theories combine to construct the elaborate and wellproportioned social edifice that macrotheorists describe?' (1983: 156). Is it possible to generalize anything at all from the perspective of organizations without ending in an abstract theory of systems or structures?

One way of conceiving the relationship between general macrotheory and theories about organizations is to look for common paradigmatic assumptions. Such an approach has been suggested by Gibson Burrell and Gareth Morgan in their book *Sociological Paradigms and Organizational Analysis*. They have been searching for 'assumptions about the nature of the social world and the way it might be investigated' (1979: x) in a variety of approaches to theories of organization. As a result of their efforts in investigating the implicit ontology and social philosophy of theories of organization, Burrell and Morgan have drawn 'a form of intellectual map'

(1979: xi) consisting of four basic paradigms representing four different philosophies of society. These paradigms are: functionalist sociology, interpretive sociology, radical humanism and radical structuralism.

Most of organization theory was found to belong to the functionalist paradigm. The discussion of functionalist organization theory takes up more than a hundred pages of the book whereas the theories of organizations belonging to the other paradigms cover only about forty pages altogether. The message of the book is a call for greater consciousness of the ontological questions among organizational theorists. I find this a sensible wish, but it is hard to follow these authors when they are arguing in favour of a 'paradigmatic closure', since the four paradigms 'stand as four mutually exclusive ways of seeing the world' (1979: 398).

In fact, remembering Jeffrey Alexander's description of the New Theoretical Movement, it seems hard to uphold the idea of mutually exclusive paradigms. According to Alexander the antifunctionalist movement has won a total victory. But the presumed functionalist organization theory is still alive. The fact that much of the organization theory Burrell and Morgan regarded as functionalist has survived the downfall of functionalist social theory seems to indicate that organization theory has a life of its own. One can criticize Burrell and Morgan on two points: first, that their idea of the four paradigms of social theory is rather artificial and hard-pressed, and second, that their linkages between the paradigms and organization theory are even more far-fetched. Perhaps there was a greater difference between the various paradigms of sociology in the sixties and the seventies, but today, at the beginning of the nineties, such an approach seems outdated. This is one of the positive contributions of the eclectic New Theoretical Movement.

Not only do Burrell and Morgan press several

organizational theorists into the functionalist camp, but they have also omitted important developments within organization theory that it would have been virtually impossible to refer to any of their paradigms (cf. Donaldson, 1985: chap. 6). Even though it may make sense to categorize some variations of organization theory as either functionalist, interpretive or radical structuralist, today one must acknowledge the fact that organization theory is as eclectic as most macrotheory and that it has liberated itself from paradigmatic dependencies. Such a statement, however, does not preclude the possibility that certain ways of theorizing about organizations are more compatible with some social philosophy than others. Maybe the social lives of organizations exceed the narrow limits of macrotheories, making those theories redundant. That is why it is important to analyse the situation of organizations in modern social landscapes. The idea of social landscapes is an alternative way of looking at the relationship between classes of social phenomena without having to fit them into a common paradigm. In social landscapes one can see how the connections between various kinds of theory regarding classes of social phenomena are determined by their very position in this landscape. This can be a way of discovering new and unexpected relations between different theoretical approaches.

Development within theories of organizations was quite rapid at the end of the seventies and the beginning of the eighties. First of all there was much criticism levelled against conventional organization theory for its conservative assumptions and its stressing of the value consensus within organizations. Some of this criticism was formulated by more or less Marxist oriented researchers. Organization theory was accused of having an asociological and ahistorical view of organizations and of reifying organizational goals and seeing them as overly rational and constrained. Moreover, organizational theory was criticized for not paying adequate attention to the existence of power relations within organizations (see Zey-Ferrell and Aiken, 1981: 1–22).

Far from being purely destructive, the new movement within theories of organizations has developed an abundance of new concepts and insights grounded in empirical investigations of organizations in action. This development has been described in books such as Richard Scott's *Organizations: Rational, Natural and Open Systems* (1981, 2nd ed. 1987) and in the third edition of Charles Perrow's *Complex Organizations: a Critical Essay*, which appeared in 1986. This is a theory of organizations that is not satisfied with studying leadership, motivation and task design. It is concerned with the growth of organizations and their power to shape their environments and how environments affect the internal life of organizations. It is a study of organizations that leaves management problems to management, concentrating upon the processes through which organizations change modern social landscapes and come to integrate ever larger parts of the social world, thereby dividing the everyday world of billions of people. I also think it is a body of theory that may be able to stand without any referents to societies or systems. The problem is that there is no single theory to use. There are a number of approaches and concepts, but it is not quite clear how they fit together.

What is organized?

How can one discern an organization in a social landscape? What distinguishes organized social life from social life in general? These are basic questions that must be tackled to realize the possibilities of analysing social development in terms of organizations. When I look out of my window I see a landscape with trees, roads and buildings. It is indeed striking that most buildings are parts of organizations and also that most organizations are in fact associated with certain kinds of building often displaying a typical architecture: steel mills, hotels, churches, prisons, hospitals. Buildings are organized, just as organizations to a large extent are physically constructed. Physical appearance is of great importance in understanding the life of the organization. Like buildings, organizations are easily discernible in all kinds of surroundings, which is not to say that the building is all there is to an organization.

Buildings are lasting structures. In the modern world people seldom build shelters for a night or two. Buildings are expected to last for quite some time. To erect a house or a factory is to make certain activities permanent. For organizations the basic feature is permanency. The first rule of organizing is: We will meet again. The basic features of organizations are individual commitments to continue, which also implies yielding to some kind of control. The means and motives of the next encounter may vary considerably but this beginning permanency is the most basic distinction between organized social life and other social activities.

One way of stating this distinction is to think in terms of markets and hierarchies. Markets are typically thought of as unorganized whereas hierarchies are the results of organizing. *Markets and Hierarchy* is also the title of a book, published in 1975, by the economist Oliver Williamson. His arguments concerning the shifts from markets to hierarchies are interesting in a discussion of the motive forces behind making social activities permanent and in understanding what is organized. Although few sociologists are likely to accept Williamson's theory in its totality, many will probably admit the fruitfulness of his approach (cf. Perrow, 1986: 241).

Williamson's theory is built upon an evaluation of transaction costs. Transactions consist of the transfer of goods or services 'across a technologically separable interface' (1981: 552). Transactions can thus be made either on a market or within organizations, in other words, through the means of hierarchy. Depending on the nature of the transaction, an actor will choose to manage his or her transactions via the market or via hierarchy according to which alternative will yield the lowest costs and the most efficient transactions. One of the most important aspects of Williamson's theory is that he admits the possibility that transactions may actually be more efficient with the use of hierarchy. In explaining the conditions that determine the costs of transactions, Williamson develops a concept: asset specificity. There are three kinds of asset specificity: physical asset specificity, site specificity, and human asset specificity (1981: 555). When there exist considerable dependencies between, for instance, a buyer and a seller in terms of any kind of asset specificity, making transactions permanent via some form of hierarchical organization will probably increase efficiency in the long run. Perhaps the most obvious example of the advantages of the hierarchical model is the transaction of labour power. In most jobs it would not be efficient to hire new labour power each day. The same goes for the supply of many kinds of raw materials. Organizing creates a permanency that eliminates some uncertainty. According to Williamson the reason behind decisions to make transactions into a permanent pattern of hierarchies is simply that it is sometimes most efficient and practical, given certain aspects of the contents of the transactions such as different kinds of asset specificity. Williamson suggests that, given certain interests, organizing is often simply the most practical solution.

There are many problems with Williamson's theory of the motive force behind organizing. One is the very idea of transaction costs. It is not easy to determine what a transaction cost is and even less easy to measure this cost in any reliable way or for any one actor involved to be able to plan transactions according to changing costs (cf. Perrow, 1986: 241–5). Williamson's ideas are unrealistic in many ways. Still, I find his principal arguments valuable for understanding commitments to organizations.

His idea of a sharp distinction between markets and hierarchies has also been questioned. Perrow argues that generally 'the distinction between markets and hierarchies is greatly overdrawn' and he reminds us that there are in fact 'strong elements of markets within hierarchies' (1986: 255). When sharply separating markets and hierarchies, one is often inclined to forget that organizations frequently fail to uphold their hierarchies. On closer scrutiny organizations can sometimes be more chaotic than a glance at their organizational chart would indicate. This is obviously true. But I will argue that when warning against an all too sharp distinction between markets and hierarchies, or organizations and their environments in general, researchers usually stress their arguments too much in favour of a non-separation between markets and hierarchies. Still, organizations do function and they hold together.

Williamson has suggested one answer to the question of what is organized: asset-specific transactions. Even if one believes that Williamson's basic idea is tenable, one could not be satisfied with this explanation as the one and only reason for organizations to exist. In his article, 'The growth of public and private bureaucracies', Marshall Meyer has underlined the importance of separating efficiency and rationality as properties of organizations. The efficiency outcomes of organizing are regarded as 'secondary to the capacity of organizations to order and to make sense of complicated environments' (1987: 215–16). Meyer argues that rationality is embedded in organizations. This is not to say that efficiency is not important, but it indicates that organizing must be understood as something more than mere efficiency. Organizing is a struggle for control and order in confrontation with a recalcitrant environment. Environments, according to Meyer, 'pose limitless uncertainty for organizations' (1987: 224). To organize is to try to overcome problems 'out there', to control them and make them work for you instead of against you. Organizations are created 'to make sense of or to rationalize environments that otherwise pose problems not admitting of solutions' (1987: 226). But organizing is a continuous endeavour, since many uncertainties surrounding organizations do not admit of definitive solutions (1987: 228). New challenges will always arise.

Organizing is a method of making human activities permanent in order to increase control over uncertain environments. Organizations detest uncertainty, as James Thompson (1967) remarked. Often enough an organization is far from successful in controlling the environment, however. This may result either in the organization vanishing, or, more commonly, in changes in the organization and a continued struggle against a hostile environment. As long as the organization persists, it constitutes a special entity in the social landscape. As James March and Herbert Simon have put it: 'the high specificity of structure and coordination within organizations – as contrasted with the diffuse and variable relations among organizations and among unorganized individuals – marks off the individual organization as a sociological unit' (1958: 4). The boundary of the organization has to do with the field over which it has control. If the essence of organizing is repeated rational control over certain aspects of human conduct, then the boundary of the organization is where this control ends. In their book *The External Control of Organizations*, Jeffrey Pfeffer and Gerald Salancik have stated: 'The organization ends where its discretion ends and another's begins.' By discretion they mean the ability to 'initiate, maintain, or end behaviors' (1978: 32).

Organizing occurs as responses to uncertain environments. It is a struggle against hostile surroundings. In the metaphorical language of landscapes, organizing may be likened to gardening, to cultivation and arrangement of the soil for the plants to grow in a controlled way. Gardening also presupposes constructing shelters against undesired unfluences from the environing landscape in the form of rain, wind, sunshine or insects. It also involves regulating nature through water and nutrient supplies. Gardening is a constant struggle to manipulate and control the environment. In the same manner organizations establish their own domains within different kinds of social landscape.

To make sure that we will meet again is to promise continued cooperation and possible lasting coordination of efforts and abilities. Continuing cooperation, however, also implies specialization and a beginning hierarchical delegation of how to coordinate behaviour. Sooner or later this process, if it continues, will generate an organization independent of the promises of individual participants. Through its hierarchy, its rules, and its artefacts and symbols, an organization becomes an extraindividual entity. This is not to say that an organization is a machine that works without human beings – on the contrary. But an organization is not constrained by the exits or entries, deaths or births, of single individuals. Individuals can always be substituted.

The relationship between organizations and individuals is paradoxical, however. On the one hand organizations have liberated themselves from a dependency on single individuals. On the other hand, the activities of organizations are tied to unique individual actors. Individual participants such as members, owners, or employees are carefully registered and their activities are measured and controlled. Just as organizations have liberated themselves from a dependency on single individuals, individual identities are extremely important within the organization.

Identities are means of control. Inside organizations the activities of individual affiliates are controlled so that they can be rewarded or punished. For the organization to persist it needs to have power over its affiliates. Organization implies having power over individual actions inside it in order to increase the control of the environment outside. Organizing may be comprehended as investment in power resources (cf. Korpi, 1985: 38).

... and what is not organized?

Organizations are centres of power and control. Much human social behaviour takes places inside organizations, but by no means all human behaviour is organized in this sense. I shall discuss this further in later sections, but to avoid misunderstanding it is necessary to touch upon the subject here. From the individual's point of view there are two kinds of social interaction that are not organized: interaction in groups and interaction among unknown people in public places.

Groups are not organized, groups happen. In groups people usually know each other: they have personal bonds. Groups are different from organizations in that they depend on individual actors. Friends are not interchangeable. Belonging to a group is not a formally recognized quality in the same way as belonging to an organization. The borders of the group are not sharp. One does not really know who belongs to a group and who does not. This is also why families are organizations and not groups. In fact, a group is a much rarer social phenomenon than one might think when reading introductory texts in sociology. It is important, though, to distinguish between groups and organizations as social entities. In their independence of individual actors organizations are qualitatively different from groups.

Relations in public are not organized either. Inter-action between people walking in the street or standing in a queue usually follows certain rules and routines. But most queues are not organized. In his book *Relations in Public* Erving Goffman has described different ways of handling public situations. He characterizes the pre-vailing rules and routines in such interaction as 'a social order'. Goffman continues: 'The study of social order is part of the study of social organization; however, a weakened notion of organization is involved' (1972: x). I would argue that it is misleading to regard these routines as organized at all. What most obviously distinguishes public situations from organized be-haviour, from the point of view of the individual, is that public situations are generally characterized by inter-action with unknown individuals. In organizations inter-action is repeated by the same identified partners. This is not the case in the street or in the queue. The social order in these situations is a quite different phenomenon from that in organizations.

In the terrain surrounding the organizational scenery there are also other kinds of social phenomena that are not organized, such as cultural processes, languages, demographic processes and gender relations. All these phenomena constitute the environment of one or several organizations. Now, it is in the nature of organizations to try to master the environment. One way of coping with the environment is to make it part of the organ-ization. This is, of course, not always possible. The environment is often resistant. Organizations are to a large extent engaged in activities, whose aim is to influence and control the nearest environment without including it in the organizations. Examples of these kinds of effort are advertising, all forms of marketing, public relations activities, policy making, temporary cooperative projects.

Customers are important actors in the terrain. Even though many customers regularly shop in the same supermarket and buy the same brand of cigarettes they are not part of the organizations in question. They are on the outside operating in a semi-organized environment. The organization has no authority over its customers although it may try to tie them to the organization in several ways, through special price reductions and other favours. On the other hand, customers do not have any ready access to influence in the organization apart from their buying behaviour. In the semi-organized field the relations between individuals and the agents of the corporate actors are asymmetrical. In asymmetrical relations the organizational actor 'controls most of the conditions surrounding the relation' (Coleman, 1982: 22).

From the point of view of the sole organization, struggling against its unpredictable and potentially hostile environment, other organizations 'out there' are part of the environment which by definition is unorganized. Everything not controlled by an organization is a source of uncertainty. This does not mean, however, that everything in the environment is chaotic. In a general sense much of what constitutes the environment for an organization is still organized. Charles Perrow has observed that actually 'the major aspect of the environment of organizations is other organizations' (1986: 177).

From an analytical perspective one organization is no more unpredictable than another. But the confrontations between the inner logic of organizations and the events that take place outside them are often of a puzzling nature for social analysis. What goes on inside organizations is quite different from what goes on between organizations or between organizations and other social phenomena.

Organizations may cooperate in many ways. There

are cartels, oligopolies and joint ventures between enterprises. There are alliances and federations between parties or nation-states. These kinds of interaction, however, are not best described as systems or structures. Cartels may be secret but they are not abstract. Co-operation between organizations becomes more intelligible in terms of what actually goes on than when they are described as systems or structures. These terms give a deceptive impression of a totality, while at the same time leaving out information about what is really going on. The interaction between organizations may thus be better comprehended in terms of networks or negotiations that go on for a certain time. And if organizations start a cooperation intended to become permanent, then it is a merger. A new and larger organization has been created, but not a system.

How is it organized?

In the previous sections of this chapter I used the terms hierarchy and authority as more or less synonymous with organizations. The basic criterion of an organization is not hierarchy, though, but affiliation. The foundation of all organizing is the registered affiliation of individuals, whose performances are controlled, recorded and remembered. In the literature on organizations, however, hierarchy and authority, perhaps along with bureaucracy, are the most common concepts used to describe what constitutes an organization and how it holds together. They are not the only concepts in this kind of analysis, though. The inner structuration of organizations has been the preoccupation of most of the research on organizations, such as questions concerning the relations between staff and line, levels of hierarchy and span of control. Most of this research has been concentrated on the formal characteristics of organizations. Their informal characteristics have gained considerable attention in certain schools of thought, however. One such approach is the study of organizational cultures.

The point of departure for all theories of organizational structure is an assumption that it is not enough to trust the members' will to manage themselves. The repetition of activities must be secured through some intrinsic measures. Demands for rationality and effectivity also make certain kinds of division of labour inevitable. Most organizing takes place through various combinations of force and incentives. Only in exceptional cases is it a question of mere coercion or mere enthusiasm.

When it comes to theorizing the exercise of authority and motivation for repeated participation, there is a peculiar lacuna in the literature. It seems as if organizational theorists do not know that people are very often paid to take part in organizations. Today one of the most frequent forms of organizational affiliation is employment. In the subject index of Richard Scott's book *Organizations: Rational, Natural and Open Systems* (1987) the words 'money', 'wages', 'employment' and 'ownership' are not to be found. It would almost appear that the word 'money' is taboo in theories of organizations. But the fact is that most authority relations in work organizations are founded on wage payments and wage differentials. Without this foundation most authority arrangements would be ineffective. In some types of organization there are of course other fundamental motives for repeated participation, for instance, in associations and interest groups.

Bureaucracy is a special kind of hierarchy with particular authority relations. It is worth noting that Max Weber in his description of the general traits of bureaucracy underlined the importance of real wages for the functioning of bureaucratic relations within an organization: an insight that seems to have been forgotten among most of his latter-day colleagues, however. A bureaucratic organization is founded on wage labour and on the career possibilities of the employees. These aspects of the organization will ensure that the employees, 'the bureaucrats', are not too interested in the content of their work and will prevent them from having a personal interest in what they are doing (1968: 958–65).

The bureaucratic model of organizing is a particular combination of hierarchy and authority. It is not the only possible combination and it is not the only form of organizing. But the concept of bureaucracy has almost become a symbol of organization. Since the work of Weber at the beginning of this century, bureaucracy has been a central topic in organizational research and many arguments have been put forward to support or criticize the idea of bureaucracy as a rational and maybe also efficient way of organizing.

Weber was no organization consultant. He was not even an organization researcher. Still, his description of the bureaucratic model of organizing has been interpreted by many as a recommendation on how to construct an ideal organization. To Weber bureaucracy was only one form, albeit an important one, of a general process of rationalization taking place in western social life. Other expressions of rationalization were science, art and architecture. The rationale of this development was, according to Weber, an aspiration to create a social life based on calculation and predictability, which was favourable to modern capitalism. The modern form of bureaucracy permeated the administration of capitalist enterprises as well as the administration of the state.

In Weber's broad historical perspective bureaucracy is the modern form of domination. It is best understood in contrast to an older form of domination, namely patriarchal domination: 'bureaucracy is merely the rational counterpart of patriarchalism' (1968: 1111). Patriarchal domination is founded on a strictly personal loyalty. Bureaucracy, on the other hand, is based on abstract and impersonal norms. Apart from dependence on wage labour and the fixed career possibilities of the employees, a bureaucratic organization relies on specialization, formal criteria of education, office hierarchy, general rules and written documents (1968: 956–8). These properties of the bureaucratic structure taken together create a kind of organizational machinery, the parts of which are human beings. The purpose of this apparatus is to secure a correspondence between top decisions and the output of the organization. The aim is to have a neutral mediation of decisions so as to create a more predictable environment for economic and social activities. The dominant qualities of bureaucracy are security and rationality rather than efficiency and speed.

Beginning with Robert Merton's well-known article of 1940, 'Bureaucratic structure and personality' (1968), there have been a number of studies expressing doubts about the value of Weber's presumed model of the ideal organization. Merton wonders if the very quality of the organization that should promote precision and reliability may not have countereffects leading to overconformity and maladjustments in a changing environment. 'But these very devices which increase the probability of conformance also lead to an over-concern with strict adherence to regulations which induces timidity, conservatism, and technicism' (1968: 255).

In his book *The Bureaucratic Phenomenon* (1964), Michel Crozier reports on his discovery of a 'bureaucratic vicious circle' in two French state organizations. Two reasons behind the development of this circle were strata isolation and parallel power relationships. The vicious circle prevented the bureaucracy from learning from its errors (1964: 186–7). Since Crozier, many researchers have found problematical breaks in organizational hierarchies such as the existence of 'loose couplings' (Weick, 1976) or 'garbage-can decision processes' (Cohen et al., 1982). The functioning of bureaucratic structures has been found to be far from perfect.

The fact that the bureaucratic structure does not run altogether up to scratch, and sometimes ends up quite wrong, does not allow us to conclude, however, that organizations do not hold together. There are many impediments to making organizations work perfectly and there are also many interests involved in an organization. Some researchers regard organizations as coalitions of interests. But these diverging interests are tied to the organization. Even if authority relations are broken and contested, new forms of agreement will evolve or else the organization will cease to exist. Organizations cannot partially hold together. They have to define their areas of authority, otherwise they will be dissolved into the environment.

Bureaucratic arrangements are not the only methods of securing permanency of behaviour in organizations. Bureaucracy can be understood as a variable (cf. Scott, 1987: 25). Authority relations can be maintained through other kinds of arrangements such as delegation of decisionmaking, in-service training, creating an internal culture, special wage arrangements.

During the last ten years or so, there has been considerable discussion of anti-hierarchical organizations. Many efforts have been made to create flexible, flat organizations with loose inner structures. Some such organizations are divisionalized forms and adhocracies (cf. Mintzberg, 1979). Another term is network organization. But these new forms of organizing, allowing freedom and initiative to individual affiliates, are still organizations. The recording of individual performances is crucial. What has made these new organizations possible is often a new technology for steering and control such as computers and telecommunications. Control has become sophisticated but it is nevertheless aimed at keeping the organization together.

Types of organization

I have argued throughout that organizations are crucial and clearly distinguishable entities within social land-scapes. On the other hand, organizations vary consider-ably in size, type of activity, and in their relationship to the environment. Still, organizing is a general process in human history with many basic similarities in all kinds of organizations. However, in order to understand and explain diverging patterns of authority and combi-nations of hierarchical mechanisms, it is necessary to analyse aspects of differences between organizations. To understand interactions between organizations and individuals, it is essential to figure out classes of basic processes between organizations and their various environments. Organizations encounter different kinds of uncertainty and react in different ways in response to changes outside the organization. Organizations also have different kinds of power resources depending on their special connections with the surrounding land-scape. To investigate the social ecology of organizations it will be necessary to consider possible typologies of organizations.

Most theorizing seems to presuppose a similarity between organizations, and most theoretical approaches claim to embrace all organizations. On the first page of their book *Organizations*, March and Simon aim to develop a theory of formal organizations, and say: 'The United States Steel Corporation is a formal organ-ization; so is the Red Cross, the corner grocery store, the New York Highway Department' (1958: 1).

March and Simon's book was published in 1958, but the tendency to generalize statements and theories of organizing to all existing organizations still seems to prevail. Even in Perrow's wide-ranging book (1986) on complex organizations not much attention is given to the problem of types of organization. But to understand what is going on between organizations and the rest of the social landscape, I think it is essential to investigate what distinguishes different kinds of organizations in terms of power resources, means of contact with individuals and with other organizations.

Despite this general tendency many efforts have been made to construct typologies of organizations for various purposes. Scott devoted a chapter of his book on organizations to an overview of varieties of organizations (1987). One obvious way of classifying organizations is to stress the kind of economic or industrial activity that predominates, be it manufacturing, construction, sales or services. This is a common way of grouping organizations in economic and socio-economic statistics. It is a classification according to the goal of the organized activities. Another, more abstract way of conceiving goals, is to use the four basic types of social function that were identified by Talcott Parsons: adaptation, goal attainment, integration, and latency. This gives four types of organization: economic, political, cultural/educational and controlling organizations. One big problem, however, in classifying organizations according to their goals is that it is often not easy to determine the goal. Many organizations have several goals and goals change over time.

Technology is of great importance for most organizations: directly, in production organizations, and more indirectly in many other organizations. One common variable in typologies according to technology is degrees of technical complexity. It was first introduced in Joan Woodward's empirical study (1965) of industrial organizations. Her results showed a clear connection between technical complexity and the internal administrative structures of the organizations. Perrow later developed the concept of complexity in terms of degrees of normality of the tasks of the organizations and of how easy it was to analyse how to handle exceptional cases. This model was also applicable in non-industrial organizations such as schools, social services or hospitals (Perrow, 1967).

In his 1984 book, *Normal Accidents*, Perrow developed another typology based on degrees of complexity. The purpose of the model is to explain why accidents can be considered normal in some organizations. Perrow separates complex and linear interactions between parts of the organization on the one hand, and tight and loose coupling between parts, on the other. The highest risk occurs in complex organizations with a tight coupling such as nuclear and chemical plants (1984: chap. 3). This is a valuable model for its purpose, but like other technological typologies it lacks connection with the social environment of the organization.

In the literature on organizations one notices a growing awareness of demands on forms of organizing that are formulated in the social and institutional environment of organizations. One of the first examples of this insight was an article published in 1977 by John Meyer and Brian Rowan, 'Institutionalized organizations: formal structure as myth and ceremony'. Meyer and Rowan argue that many of the internal forms and practices of organizations are there only to satisfy the demands of an institutionalized environment. This conformity to institutionalized rules may in fact often hinder efficiency. The reason they are adopted is to increase the legitimacy of the organizations. Organizations, thus, 'reflect the myths of their institutional environments instead of the demands of their work activities' (1977: 341; cf. Meyer et al., 1987). The idea of an 'institutional isomorphism' has been developed by Paul DiMaggio and Walter Powell, who identify three mechanisms of isomorphic demands on organizations. Isomorphism may be either coercive, mimetic or normative depending on the motive behind the adoption of ideas and myths concerning how to organize properly (1983: 150). The idea of an institutional pressure on most organizations is a way of understanding social relations between organizations. It is also a way of saying that the environment is not all that uncertain. There are very plain signals as well.

In a discussion on the organization of societal sectors Richard Scott and John Meyer have combined the existence of institutional demands with the level of technical development into a theoretically comprehensive typology. Thus, organizations can be exposed to strong institutional demands but weak technical demands, for instance, schools or social welfare organizations, or there can be strong technical demands and a weak pressure from the institutional environment, which is the situation for most manufacturing organizations, at least in the United States. There are also organizations that are exposed to strong technical and institutional demands, such as hospitals and banks. And there are some organizations that are comparatively free of both technical and institutional demands, such as personal service organizations. These organizations tend to be relatively small (1983: 140–1; see also Scott, 1987: 126–7). The various combinations of technical and institutional demands are important for understanding both the internal structures of organizations and their chances of survival and growth as well as their power resources. Still, there are many dimensions missing in the model, for instance the relationship to individuals. This is a most significant dimension if one is to apply a typology of organizational sectors in a discussion of the micro–macro problem in social theory. In his 1961 book, *A Comparative Analysis of Complex Organizations*, Amitai Etzioni addressed the question of organizations as mechanisms of social order mediating between individuals and the social structure. The comparative analysis consists of a typology describing different forms of relationship between individuals and organizations.

The basis for Etzioni's typology is the nature of compliance in the organization, which has to do with both the processes of power within the organization and the type of involvement of individuals in the organization. From the nine possible types of organization yielded by this classification, Etzioni distinguishes three as 'congruent types' (1961: 12–14). These are called coercive, utilitarian and normative organizations. Coercive means of power in an organization are assumed to correspond to an alienating involvement. Utilitarian organizations employ remunerative means of power and display a calculative involvement, whereas normative organizations are founded on a moral kind of involvement. Prisons are examples of coercive organizations. Manufacturing industries are utilitarian and labour unions or religious organizations are normative.

I find Etzioni's compliance model very interesting. It is also unique in its way of connecting organizations and their relations to individuals with models of social structures. I also think that his way of classifying means of power is sensible, albeit a little vague. When it comes to analysing involvement, however, the classification becomes much too vague and arbitrary. That the involvement in coercive organizations is alienating is not difficult to understand, but to distinguish between utilitarian and moral involvement seems to be a delicate task, as is displayed in Etzioni's discussion of different kinds of political organization (1961: 76–7).

Individuals, organizations and social landscapes

Organizations are arrangements to make permanent, coordinate and control aspects of human behaviour in order to try to ensure mastery over uncertain environments. I have argued that organizations have a central role in relation to the theoretical problem of a micro-macro link. There is no macrostructure above organizations. Individual actors confront 'society' in the form of organizations. The practical consciousness of individuals may be routinized in Giddens' terminology, but the important point is that most routines are formalized into organizational arrangements. This does not imply that individuals have no choices towards organizations. They have. I shall discuss this in Chapter 3.

There are many words to designate the relationship between individuals and organizations in particular situations: member, customer, client, employee, patient, prisoner, inmate, student, citizen, owner, spectator, subscriber, passenger etc. There is no one term, however, to describe this relationship universally. In his discussion of the compliance structures of organizations, Etzioni has taken up the question of 'lower participants and organizational boundaries'. He has distinguished three dimensions referring to lower participants: nature of involvement, subordination, and performance obligations. To be a participant, Etzioni argues, it is necessary to score highly 'on at least one of the three dimensions of participation' (1961: 21). Consequently, he does not regard customers or clients as participants. This is contrary to, for instance, the approach of March and Simon, who regard consumers and suppliers as participants in business organizations (1958: 89). On this point I wholly agree with Etzioni. It is essential to have some criteria that designate a more permanent commitment towards the organizations when defining participants or affiliates. Individual affiliations to organizations are the basic connections between organizations and everyday life.

Being an affiliate entails both obligations and rights, having a commitment, being subject to the internal rules of the organization, and belonging within its internal authority structure. It further means acquiring an organizational identity and a recorded history of performances within the organization. These preconditions for being an affiliate or part of an organization exclude relationships between organizations and individuals such as customers, spectators or subscribers. Even if a subscriber may be considered to have a regular relationship with an organization, this does not imply any commitments or rights to an internal position of any kind. This definition includes relationships such as patients, students, prisoners, employees, and members. I shall also argue that citizenship, ownership, and kinship are relations of the same kind, implying a status of affiliation in an organization.

This definition of affiliation is in line with Etzioni's definition of lower participants, the greatest difference being that this model includes not only lower participants but 'higher' participants as well. Thus, it stresses not only obligations and subordination but also members' and owners' rights to take part in decisions. Moreover, I think the term affiliate is more accurate than the term participant, because it emphasizes the formal aspects of being part of an organization. Being organized is a formal relationship.

Still, being a customer or a passenger implies a relationship with an organization even though it is not as part of it. I shall argue that the connections between, say, customers and an organization take place in a semi-organized field.

Affiliation is a formal category. One is either an affiliate or not. There are many ways of acquiring an affiliation as I have defined the term here. One can pay a fee to become member of a club or a union or one can take on employment or be imprisoned. Considering affiliation in this sense, there is one striking distinction which seems fundamental in comprehending the relations between individuals and organizations. Affiliation can be either compulsory or voluntary. The distinction between compulsory and voluntary affiliation is quite clear and simple and yet it is of the utmost importance for understanding how individuals and organizations interact. To be an owner or an employee of a business enterprise or to be a member of a union or a political party is a voluntary engagement. Circumstances such as risks of unemployment or lack of opportunities to move can prevent someone from leaving employment, but there is nothing in the organization to stop a person from quitting. There may be some extraordinary organizations where one can enter voluntarily but may not leave, such as monastic orders. But these are rare exceptions.

On the other hand, one is born into being a citizen of a nation-state and being a member of a family and it is very difficult to change these relations. There are strict rules for changing citizenship or being adopted into another family. It is virtually impossible not to be a citizen or a member of a family. These are compulsory and enforced relationships between individuals and organizations.

The distinction between voluntary and compulsory affiliation to organizations is fundamental. It implies differences in the kinds of involvement of individuals as well as in the kinds of power resources the organizations may employ. It is a comprehensive distinction that involves very broad categories of organizations. In this connection it is important to realize that kinship is actually a form of organization with hierarchical implications. Moreover, it is probably the oldest organizational form in human history. Despite its comprehensiveness, the distinction between organizations founded on voluntary affiliation and those presupposing complusory affiliation is unusually plain and clear-cut. It does not exclude other kinds of distinction concerning affiliation, but it must be considered one of the basic distinctions in any broad typology of organizational sectors.

The inclusion of citizenship and kinship as concepts denoting affiliation to an organization can in some ways be considered an extension of the idea of what organizations are. Sociologists sometimes distinguish between organizations and institutions. The state and the family are often regarded as institutions. But I find it only confusing to make this distinction. One should talk about either institutions or organizations, but not both. For understanding interactions between individuals it is of fundamental importance whether these interactions occur inside or outside organizations. And in this respect families and nation-states are similar to other forms of organization.

The importance of separating human interaction inside and outside organizations was brought out by Hans Gerth and C. Wright Mills in their book *Character and Social Structure*, although they use the concept of institution. Gerth and Mills distinguish five institutional orders: political, economic, military, kinship and religious orders. They also discuss the differences between voluntary associations and compulsory institutions (1970: 24–6). The same distinction was made earlier by Weber (1968: 52). The weakness in the classification of institutional orders by Gerth and Mills, however, is that they mix formal and functional categories. I maintain, on the other hand, that a categorization of organizations must be strictly formal, taking into consideration only how organizations are constituted and not what kind of activity they are involved in, since that is a secondary matter and can vary across organizations. There is no necessary connection between organizational form and type of activity.

Compulsory relations to organizations are not easily explained in terms of efficiency and transaction costs. From the point of view of the organization, though, compulsory affiliations may be comprehended as forms of rationality. The problem of 'free riders' is, in principle, non-existent in organizations with compulsory membership, such as nation-states or families. Obligations such as military service or tax payment do not allow free riders. This is the difference between paying taxes and paying fees to a trade union. Compulsory affiliation is a way of overcoming the uncertainty created by free riders. Of course, people may try to withhold their income, for instance, to avoid taxation. But that is against the rules. Free riders do not break any rules.

I have argued that it is misleading to regard societies or systems as superunits. Organizations of different kinds do not fit together into a system with a special logic of power and determination. They are not tied together at the top. Instead they lead their own lives, pulling and struggling in various directions as they try to master their environment. Neither is there any general institutional environment that confronts all organizations. Organizations of various sorts constitute the institutional environment for each other. But different kinds of organization have particular preconditions for their interaction with other organizations.

Organizations interact with each other in several ways: doing business, engaging in politics, negotiating, making war. These interactions take place in different kinds of terrain. The typical terrain for doing business is the market, where organizations interact to sell and buy each other's products. A basic feature of this interaction is circulation. A market needs new products and new combinations of buyers and sellers. For business organizations to succeed it is essential to be mobile. Warfare is another kind of interaction between organizations. A war is a matter of territorial control. Wars are typically fought between nation-states controlling and defending certain territories.

These examples indicate that the spatial connections of organizations are important for understanding their interaction. Whether organizations are mobile or stable is crucial for analysing their power resources and their strategies for survival and growth. When focusing on the spatial connections of organizations it becomes evident that this is a very clear area of difference between types of organization. Capitalist enterprises are mobile. They have no territory to defend. In fact, one of the most important aspects of the development of capitalist enterprises is their mobility: the establishment of new industries or the search for new customers. Unprofitable industries are closed down and left behind. Sites are bought and sold. Capitalist enterprises do not lay out any boundaries and they do not, in principle, have any geographical ties. Of course, at certain points in time an enterprise may be tied to an industrial establishment or to a natural site, for instance, a mine or a forest. But the location is not the essence of the organization, which is capital, and capital is relatively easy to move around.

Nation-states, on the other hand, are defined according to their territories, their borders being among their most fundamental characteristics. Nation-states can grow or become reduced in terms of area covered, but they cannot move. They are tied to their core territory. The territorial aspect is what unites the nation-state when it comes to such fundamental activities as military actions, taxation, construction of roads or building of schools. The organization of these activities is based on geographical districts such as provinces and municipalities. The territorial dimension permeates all the organizational arrangements of the nation-state. The nation-state organization is large, but it has to cover every corner of its territory. The nation-state organization comprises all public authorities within its territory, including organizations such as the postal administration, in one unit.

When describing voluntary associations such as trade unions, political parties, or sport clubs, it is striking that all of them have some kind of district organization. The territorial connection is of great importance for understanding the development of voluntary associations that depend on the activities of their members for their existence. The cooperation and coordination of these activities are dependent on a territorial base for the arrangement of meetings or outward actions. Members are defined according to their spatial positions, be it a town, a province or a particular work site, and divided into local branches of the organization. Such an organization cannot move far away from its members. Unlike the nation-state, however, it may cease to exist. The territorial aspect of voluntary organizations is very important even if it is not as fundamental as in the case of nation-states. Voluntary organizations are generally immobile and this immobility is a significant factor in explaining their strategies and activities vis-a-vis their environment, for instance in understanding the power relations between trade unions and multinational enterprises.

Kinship relations, on the other hand, are not dependent on a territorial connection. Families, or kinship organizations, may persist in many kinds of terrain and family relations are maintained for generations despite the fact that certain members have been highly mobile. There are many historical and current examples of 'multinational' families such as royal houses, merchants or immigrants. The family ties are upheld through heritage and economic transactions of various kinds and also through ritual ceremonies such as funerals or weddings. Of course, there are families with close links

to certain territories through, for instance, the ownership of land. The point is, however, that these connections are not necessary for the family organization to
survive.

Historically the importance of families and kinship
organizations in social life is declining. In the social
landscape families are being superseded by other types
of organization. Families are no longer production units
to the same extent. They survive, however, as important
units for consumption, upbringing and affection.
Families are built on authority at least as regards the
relations between parents and children before they
leave the home. The signs of dissolution of the family
have been exaggerated. Family and kinship are still
essential organizational units in the social world.

Thus organizations are based in everyday life through
their connections to individual affiliates. Their bonds
are of a different character, however, depending on
whether individual affiliation is voluntary or compulsory
and whether their affiliates are spatially defined or not.
Thus, individuals are connected to organizations
through compulsory or voluntary affiliation and the
interaction of organizations is conditioned by their
spatial connections in the social landscape. Combining
these categories will yield four types of organization:
capitalist enterprises, voluntary associations, nation-
states and families. These are the four primary types of
organization. Capitalist enterprises are mobile. Their
primary voluntary form of affiliation is ownership.
Voluntary associations are spatially stable organizations
with voluntary membership. Nation-states are stable
with a compulsory affiliation in the form of citizenship.
Families are mobile organizations based on kinship
relations. Moreover, all four types of organization have
a secondary form of affiliation, namely, employment.

The qualities I have distinguished, which are displayed
in Figure 1, are of basic importance for understanding

	Capitalist enterprises	Voluntary associations	Nation-states	Families
Mode of primary affiliation	voluntary	voluntary	compulsory	compulsory
Spatial connection	loose mobile	tight stable	tight stable	loose mobile
Form of primary affiliation	ownership	membership	citizenship	kinship
Form of secondary affiliation	employment	employment	employment	employment
Tasks	special	special	general	general
Mode of access	private	public	public	private
Primary power structure	ownership	participatory structure	political structure	genera-tions

Figure 1 Characteristics of four organizational sectors

how organizations survive and grow and how they affect their environment. This is not to say that these qualities are the most important properties in describing the nature of each organizational sector. To understand the mechanisms of capitalism or the nature of families as organizations it is necessary to take other conditions into consideration as well, conditions that are distinctive for each type of organization. But I maintain that these basic qualities of organizations are of great importance in comparing types of organizations and their interaction with each other and with individuals in the social landscape.

The organizational scenery is changing all the time. Specific organizations may change their character; voluntary organizations may become compulsory state organizations or they may become capitalist enterprises. There are transitions going on between organizational sectors, but at any one point the greater part of any organization will belong to one of these four sectors. When organizations change sector they also change character. This typology, however, does not cover historical forms of organizing such as slavery or serfdom.

There are many possible forms of intertwinement between these four organizational sectors, between the nation-state and capitalist enterprises, between voluntary organizations and the nation-state, between capitalist enterprises and families, or between families and the nation-state. But the important point and reason behind the distinction of organizations into organizational sectors is that these forms of intertwinement may be understood rather as interactions between different entities than as internal processes within a society or a system. The anomalies and unexpected events in these processes are better comprehended as encounters between strangers than as processes between parts of a whole.

From the classification of organizational sectors according to forms of affiliation and spatial connections, it is possible to make further generalizations about the operations of different kinds of organization.

The contrast between voluntary and compulsory membership is essential for understanding the relations between individuals and organizations. Compulsory affiliation yields a more durable relationship. Individuals cannot change organization, but the organization cannot get rid of its members either. This has consequences, for example, when it comes to the tasks an organization will be engaged in. Compulsory affiliation means greater dependency between individuals and organizations, and therefore stronger ties between them. This implies both that the organization has a stronger grip on its affiliates and that affiliates may make stronger demands on the organization.

Marshall Meyer has argued, as a criticism of Weber, that 'the idea of rational administration could not be transferred from business to government' (1985: 26). The simple reason is that public agencies 'are more likely than other types of organizations to have tasks that are not easily accomplished or whose accomplishment is not easily measured' (1985: 5). The strong ties between members and organizations in nation-states as well as in families will sometimes make it possible for members to make extensive demands for help and service from the organization which are not always easy to fulfil. It is harder for an organization with compulsory affiliation to avoid certain difficult tasks, than for an organization with voluntary affiliation. These latter organizations may choose not to do certain things, and also ask the affiliates to go somewhere else. In this way organizations with compulsory affiliation may be said to deal with general tasks, wheras organizations with voluntary affiliation only deal with special tasks of their own choosing. Nation-states as well as families may have to fulfil a broad variety of functions for their affiliates, while capitalist enterprises and voluntary organizations can specialize in what they do best.

But the strong links between affiliates and organization also imply stronger demands from the organization on its affiliates, which are connected with stricter control and more far-reaching power measures. Both capitalist enterprises and voluntary associations have to motivate their members to stay in the organization, which does not prevent them from sometimes using strict control and discipline inside the organization. In the end, though, the affiliates of these organizations can choose to stay in the organization or leave it. Compulsory organizations, on the other hand, do not usually have to worry about whether their affiliates will remain in the organization or not. But they cannot dispose of their affiliates, either, except through extreme measures such as killing them. They will use stronger means of influence and control for correcting behaviour than voluntary organizations. If nation-states could simply dismiss certain affiliates, they would not need the monopoly of physical violence. Behind organizational arrangements in the nation-state such as taxation, military service, compulsory schooling and law enforcement in general, there is always the threat of physical violence. Families also have strong means of control, particularly in the relations between parents and children. Even if parents do not beat their children regularly, they still have a strong physical advantage over them. In the process of upbringing, parents have large amounts of authority and control. In many families the existence of family property and heritage are effective power resources.

The spatial connections of organizations are related to their degrees of openness. Spatially stable organizations are in principle public, whereas organizations that are mobile have a private mode of access. In public organizations affiliation is open to everybody within a territory, provided they fulfil certain conditions. In private organizations access is much more limited.

The sources of power and rights of decisionmaking inside organizations are connected with primary affiliation. All kinds of primary affiliates have access to some forms of representation in decisionmaking. Even if they have no real influence, they are to be reckoned with. In capitalist enterprises the power structure is rooted in forms of ownership. In voluntary organizations the basis of power is participation in meetings and activities. In nation-states primary decisionmaking is arranged into political processes of varying form (they need not be democratic processes). In families power is distributed primarily along generations.

The formal processes of decisionmaking among primary affiliates of organizations are, however, rarely descriptions of the actual decisionmaking in organizations at work. Still, I find it important to distinguish these basic sources of power. In all organizational sectors there is a secondary affiliation based on employment. The ratio between the number of affiliates and the number of employees is in most cases very different between different organizational sectors. In capitalist enterprises the number of employees normally exceeds the number of owners many times over. In voluntary associations, as well as in nation-states, on the other hand, the number of affiliates considerably exceeds the number of employees. In families, finally, employees are unusual, and if there are any they will normally be fewer in number than the family members themselves. In nation-states and in families, moreover, there is an anomaly between primary affiliation, which is compulsory, and secondary affiliation, which is voluntary.

In many cases primary and secondary affiliation overlap. Employees are sometimes part-owners of capitalist enterprises. In the nation-state, in fact, most employees are also citizens. In voluntary associations members may be employed as officials or representatives. In families this is very unlikely to happen, however. Still, it is important to separate primary and secondary affiliation when it comes to power resources and ways of exercising power. The power resources of affiliates are connected with the particular form of affiliation, whereas the main source of power of employees is their knowledge of the practical routines of the organization.

From the start employees are not meant to have any decisive power resources concerning strategic decisions in organizations. But as several classical studies within the social sciences have shown, employees will gradually acquire fairly important power positions in organizations. This is the implication of expressions such as 'the iron law of oligarchy' or 'the managerial revolution'. In this way organizations tend to become coalitions of two or more interest groups. At the same time the processes of decisionmaking will become more complex.

The distinction between compulsory and voluntary affiliation applies only to primary affiliates; employment is always voluntary. Still, it is important to regard employees as part of the organization. Employees have permanent connections with the organization and they belong to its internal authority structure, in contrast to the subscribers to a newspaper or sympathizers with a political party. In all organizations there are, in fact, strict definitions to separate primary and secondary affiliates, on the one hand, and other parties interested in the particular activities of the organization, on the other. When talking about coalitions of interest groups in organizations, I think it is essential to draw a sharp line between those who really belong to the organization and groups outside it. This was not done by Richard Cyert and James March in their well-known analysis of organizational coalitions (1963: 27).

Inside the organization individual activities are reasonably well controlled and predicted. Total control is impossible. Outside the organization, on the other hand, there is often a zone of what will be called a semi-organized field, where an organization tries to control the operations of individuals or other organizations through marketing, public relations, propaganda, negotiations, etc. These efforts, however, are very different in character from the processes of control within the organization. Inside organizations individuals are identified and their performances are recorded. Outside organizations they operate in anonymity.

Social life is not limited to what happens inside the four organizational sectors. Outside organizations several kinds of activity which shape the social world go on among individuals or groups of individuals. Some of the more essential social phenomena that are not primarily organized are cultural processes, languages, traditions, status systems, gender relations, ethnicity. Through individual affiliates these phenomena may influence the organizational structure and its operations to varying degrees. However, organizations also try to transform the environment to suit their purposes. There is a tendency for culture and similar unorganized phenomena to be drawn into the semi-organized field in the form of politics, art or marketing, for instance. It seems that there is, in the modern world, an increasing movement towards organizing. More and more social activities will take place inside organizations or in the semi-organized field.

The organizational scenery and the social world

The organizational scenery is not an unbounded mass of social activities. In fact, it is comparatively easy to distinguish one organization from another. The activities of organizations are normally planned and documented and their affiliates are registered and counted. The semi-organized field, however, is more diffuse and is spreading further out into the surrounding terrain through modern means of communication. But the organizations themselves are fairly easy to recognize and their boundaries are relatively distinct. This argument does not imply that organizations are closed, rigid entities, nor that life within organizations always goes on as planned. The boundaries and activities of organizations may change rapidly and the outcome of their activities may be unexpected. The point is, however, that at any one point an organization is a clearly defined entity and its activities are separated distinctly from the environment. In comparison with concepts like systems, structures, or societies, organizations are concrete and discernible. Thus, they are easier to handle in social analysis. Thinking in terms of organizations will generate a clearer notion of what is really going on and how the relations with individual actors are maintained. It will give a less mystifying idea of the positions of individuals in social life. One cannot be affiliated to a system.

But don't social scientists need concepts like systems or societies? I don't think so, at least, not any longer. It was probably meaningful to divide the world of two hundred years ago into separate societies. Today, however, it is not possible to tell where one society ends and another begins. Very often nations are regarded as societies. But nations are not unitary societies any more. A nation-state is a type of organization, but nations as delimited entities simply do not exist any longer. Nation-states are not superimposed on the other organizational sectors. National territories are permeated by a multitude of processes stretching far beyond their geographical boundaries. This development makes it impossible to talk about separate societies or systems. That is why the concepts of system and society have become superfluous in social analysis. To think in terms of systems or societies is to try to make totalities out of processes that intertwine and overlap to such an extent that it is virtually impossible to tell where one system ends and another begins.

All efforts to delimit a system must be arbitrary or artificial. It is like painting a landscape. The artist has chosen a perspective and a certain place to put up his easel to fit his intentions and emotions. In this way an artist creates a totality of forms and colours that may be interpreted as internal relations within the picture. A landscape may be painted as a delimited unit, but in reality the landscape never ends. It covers the whole of the earth. And it is exactly the same with the social landscape. It ends where human life ends. All social life on earth is bound together. On this scale one may talk about a totality of social life, but that is the only social totality that exists.

As a totality all social life on earth is related to other parts of social life. It is hardly an organic totality, though. The totality of the social world cannot be split up into parts that fit neatly together, constituting the whole. It is rather a forced totality pressed together within its global confines. It is an unordered, almost chaotic, totality of social life consisting of parts competing with each other, with different means of power for control over human and natural resources.

Among the more substantial parts in this one totality are the four organizational sectors I have distinguished. Within the sectors these organizations operate in different places, but across the four sectors they overlap. Capitalist enterprises often stretch their activities across several nation-states. Trade unions penetrate the areas of many enterprises. Members of the same family may be citizens of different nation-states.

The four types of organization have varying possibilities and restrictions for movements across the social landscape and have different types of relations wih their affiliates. These conditions are decisive for the interaction between organizations from different sectors within the social world. It is also the case that the organizations within each sector and across sectors presuppose each other to a large extent. Trade unions would hardly exist if there had not been any capitalist enterprises; the three other sectors are all to a high degree dependent on nation-states for certain aspects of their activities. Still, these interdependencies do not make them into societies, because the interdependencies do not add up into wholes.

But don't all organizations within one sector make up

a system? If system only means that there are many organizations of the same kind, one can perhaps say that an organizational sector is a system. It may make sense to say that all the capitalist enterprises make up a capitalist system. This is a very weak notion of system, however, which implies only that organizations within the same sector interact with each other.

The organizational scenery does not yet cover the whole of the social world. Organizations are spread out in the social landscape in varying combinations, for instance, cities and villages. Organizations of different sectors are mixed into geographically located units and encounters between organizations take place in many kinds of terrain. The appearance of the terrain is important for understanding the outcome of organizational encounters and interaction. In the terrain there are also individuals.

3
The Individual Domain

Organizations in everyday life

Most people spend the greater part of their time and their everyday life inside organizations of various types. At home, at work, at school, playing soccer with the team or going to a union meeting you take your place in an organization. This means that you know your place, you know what you have to do and who will complain and take action if you don't. You are expected to arrive around a certain time and stay for an agreed length of time. You know the people you meet, at least by name (or perhaps number) and position, and you know what you can ask of them. You have met them before and you will meet them again. In the organization you have an identity and a record.

But there is also social life outside organizations. You take the bus or the train to work; after work you may go shopping or to a restaurant, watch sport or visit a museum. All these activities take place in the semi-organized field. What they have in common is that they are connected to organizations of various types. The activity in question is arranged by an organization, which also supplies the objects for what you want to do. But in your relations with organizations in the semi-organized field you are normally not known, you are anonymous and not expected to state who you are. Your only time restriction is to come when it is open. You can generally choose from several places to go shopping or to eat. When you are going home or to work there are no choices. In the bus or in the train on the way to work you may recognize a few people whom you have seen almost every workday for several years. But you may not know their names and you don't expect anything of them.

After work, if you don't have too many duties at home, you may have some time to spend outside your organizational realms, to go and see friends perhaps. You don't have to go, but there seem to be longer and longer intervals between the times you see each other. The old gang is diminishing. So you feel you should go. There is a risk that the group will be dissolved. Unfortunately, there is an important meeting at the local union where your presence is important. On your way to the union meeting you may meet a neighbour, with whom you stop for a chat about the weather, but being in a hurry you have to make your excuses and leave your neighbour. Still, you felt you had to say a few words.

In this way the everyday world is divided between different organizational sojourns and the trips between them. But organizational bonds are not limited to certain places. From work you may be able to call your spouse or your children on the telephone to decide family matters. When at home you may extend your contacts with your family through long-distance calls to parents or children who live far away. New technology has made it easier for families to hold together over long distances. Illiterate women in rural villages in the Middle East send tape recordings of their family life to their husbands working in the oil fields of Saudi Arabia.

When you are watching TV in your living-room with your family, you also take your position in the semi-organized fields of the various TV channels: a position that you may share with millions of people all around the world. But you are not participating in any way and you are totally anonymous. The everyday world is permeated by various organizational arrangements. Your organizational affiliations dominate your life, but not all your life, and there are choices.

Passing through the social landscape you first see organizations from the outside. A stranger or a traveller will first notice the semi-organized field, shops, restaurants, advertisements, propaganda, signs and symbols. The semi-organized field is often loud and lively; visibility is essential. Semi-organized fields are often described as markets, and tourism is travelling in the semi-organized field. It is hard for a stranger, however, to see the inside of organizations. The entrances of organizations are mostly insignificant and also protected. Compare the main entrance of a big department store with its staff entrance. The organizational power centres are hidden. Only the affiliates know the way.

People's organizational affiliations are, however, sometimes apparent to the outsider through clothes or other symbolic outfits. Some affiliates of the nation-state have to wear uniforms, for instance, schoolchildren, military or police. Many enterprises equip their employees with jackets, overalls or headgear in certain colours with the company name or logo printed on them. Members of voluntary organizations such as political parties, sports clubs, or youth organizations wear special clothes to announce that they belong to the organization. This is another aspect of the presence of organizations in the social landscape.

From birth every human being is affiliated to a family and a nation-state. Children's first experiences of the exercise of power occur within the family. After some years all children will have to yield to the power of the nation-state in the form of school. Growing up, children will slowly get to know the world outside the family and the school. Gradually the everyday world will be larger, adolescence being the typical time for activities in groups or gangs of various kinds. It is an organizational interregnum. Having married and settled down and started to work, people fill their everyday lives again with organizational affiliations. In the course of their lives individuals orient themselves within the existing organizations in the social landscape. Every individual attempts to establish a domain within this landscape, balancing between different organizational influences and leaving some unorganized space.

Organizations are power centres. They accumulate power and they have a tendency to try to increase their control. From the perspective of individuals, organizations may be experienced as centrifugal powers threatening to divide and disintegrate the balance between organizational influences in everyday life. Capitalist enterprises, the nation-state, voluntary organizations and your family all make demands on your time and on your place in the social landscape. The semi-organized fields are increasing their scope.

Organizations are not only threats, though. They are also opportunities. That is their attraction. They offer activities and various kinds of reward. They give you protection and strength. But enjoying the advantages that most organizations can offer always implies surrendering to demands and control. Organizations give you tasks to do and an identity, but also duties. Freedom from organization is anonymity.

Organizations do not only propagate and advertise. More important, they arrange events and routines. They offer premises for activities, churches, sports arenas, theatres, factories, schools, homes. They not only influence people, but also make them do things. They also monopolize activities. Phenomena such as art, religion, work are not comprehensible today outside their organizational realms. Art is all that is sold in art galleries or exhibited in museums. Religion is what is practised in churches, mosques or temples. Work is what is done as wage labour within organizations.

Social life is reproduced and also changed in an interplay between organizations and individual actors. If, at any time, there is a social order, it is upheld by organizations and not by societal systems or structures. Likewise, democratic processes and other forms of decisionmaking and communicative action are better comprehended in relation to specific organizational sectors than to abstruse systems.

Even if organizations are able to concentrate power resources, they do not have all the power. They do not determine everything that goes on in the social world. Individual actors can influence organizations. In this chapter I shall investigate some concepts for analysing individual behaviour and strategies vis-a-vis organizations and their applicability in different sorts of terrain in order to facilitate an analysis of the limits of organizational power.

Movements among multiple realities

The spatial perspective on social analysis which is explicit in the metaphor of the social landscape has many sources and origins. In Chapter 1 I mentioned the criticism levelled against social scientists by several geographers. There are many surprising similarities between some of these geographical approaches to social analysis and the phenomenological view of social reality. In phenomenology space and time are essential categories for describing the position of individuals in social life. Much of the inspiration for the uses of phenomenology in the social sciences comes from the German philosopher and social scientist Alfred Schutz, who moved to the United States during the Second World War. In his famous article 'On multiple realities' he writes that 'the wide-awake man' 'is primarily interested in that sector of the world of his everyday life which is within his scope and which is centered in space and time around himself' (Schutz 1962: 222).

Now, what Schutz offers is a terminology and a way of accounting for how individual actors perceive the intersubjective world around them and how they try to handle this world. The starting point for Schutz is the social world which existed long before each individual became aware of it. 'Now it is given to our experience and interpretations,' says Schutz (1962: 208). It is for each individual to make sense of the objective social world as best he or she can. In so doing, however, individuals necessarily also change the world. But the objects of the world will offer resistance to change which must be overcome, or else one has to yield to the given reality.

The individual orients himself in the world of multiple realities through his 'bodily movements'. The world is explored and experienced through the body and its senses, through personal encounters with the objective world. The 'finite provinces of meaning' each individual has are created by working in and upon the social world through personal experience of what is going on. This is not to deny the importance of socialization and previous knowledge. No one starts from zero. But, as I understand it, the important point is that the knowledge and experience that the individual has acquired through education and socialization is always reinterpretable in the light of new experiences. And these new experiences are made and understood in relation to the bodily movements around a sector of the social world. Even if many people have similar experiences of the social world, these experiences are always unique to each individual. On the other hand, Schutz also stresses that it is impossible to derive any meaning from social life without expectations of what is going to happen. All new events are interpreted and comprehended in relation to previous ones.

The individual domain is that 'segment of the world which is pragmatically relevant' (1962: 213). Every individual has their own segment, their own combination of relevant pieces which they put together into their own everyday routines with a particular finite province of meaning. There is no ready formula on how to act in every segment of the world with its unique combination of elements. Everybody has to find their own way to the bus. Making up this pragmatic world-view implies using very many different kinds of information, mixing gossip, official news, advice from friends and relatives together with one's own observations. The main point in Schutz's theory is 'the predominance of the manipulatory area'. This means that 'the world of our working, of bodily movements, of manipulating objects and handling things and men constitutes the specific reality of everyday life' (1962: 223).

The spatial nature of the relationship between man and his everyday world is underlined by the expression 'the world within his reach', which denotes 'the kernel of his social reality' (1962: 224). The everyday world is kept together by locomotions and communications, which may extend over long distances through modern technology. For some people the everyday world may include several airports of the world and contacts with the stock markets in both Hong Kong and New York.

There is a touch of the frontier spirit in Schutz's perspective. Everybody is an explorer of his own everyday world. Within the limits of the bodily movements the social world is there to discover. Schutz's perspective of social life is in many ways attractive and, I think, also rather fruitful. It gives a general notion of how to perceive the position of individuals in the social landscape. At the same time, however, the value of this perspective is limited in its extreme individuality.

Even though Schutz mentions that the objects of the social world will offer resistance, the absence of any notions of power or contradictions in the social world is a conspicuous flaw in his social philosophy. He has nothing to say about the dynamics of the social world. Without any connections with what is going on in the social world his concepts of bodily movements and the world within one's reach become too general. However, what is important is his emphasis on the connections between personal experiences of events and the interpretation of the immediate social world.

If the social world may be likened to a labyrinth of multiple realities, incomprehensible to individual actors, it must be added that it is a labyrinth with no way out. There is no single constructor of this labyrinth, there are many. And none of them has any final responsibility. None of the paths will lead to the goal. All paths are sooner or later barred by later constructions. The social world has few open horizons.

The seriality of everyday life

From a similar phenomenological perspective, Jean-Paul Sartre, in his *Critique of Dialectical Reason* (1976), investigates the relations between individuals and the social world. Sartre offers a grandiose social philosophy which is quite problematic in its totality. Some of the concepts developed by Sartre are useful, however, for the analysis of relations between individuals and organizations in the social landscape. In particular, I shall discuss his ideas on seriality and on the practico-inert field.

If the social world according to Alfred Schutz seemed somewhat idyllic, it is more threatening and nasty in Sartre's perspective. Power and contradiction have no place in Schutz's theory, but in Sartre's social philosophy they are essential. Like Schutz, Sartre starts from the two poles of the individual and the social world, but in his social reality the objective world plays a more active role, since it is also the product of individuals, but, alas, other individuals. A central aphorism in Sartre's social philosophy is: 'But if History escapes me, this is not because I do not make it; it is because the other is making it as well' (1968: 88). This is Sartre's way of addressing the problem of the unintended consequences of human action. Sartre writes about 'counter-finality' (1976: 164). Even if things don't go your way it is not because you are not struggling hard enough or that you don't know what to do. The others are also struggling hard and know a lot. Still, it is not necessarily true that the others are consciously struggling against you. You may not even be aware of them. What the others do is mediated to you through the practico-inert field. And in the world today there are many others; they can be counted in billions.

In Schutz's theory there seemed to be a clear distance between the individual and the social world, while according to Sartre the individual is always embedded in social reality. The individual is not alone.

Sartre amply demonstrates the impossibility of a social analysis based on either individualism or the dyadic relationship. For him the basis of social life rests upon the triad. 'Reciprocal ternary relations are the basis of *all* relations between men, whatever form they may subsequently take' (Sartre, 1976: 111). The stressing and enhancing of the trinary nature of all relationships is a way of discovering latent contradictions in all social situations, even the simplest everyday routines. The idea of the triad stems from the realization of the absurdity of an individualistic or dyadic approach. It is simply a fact that in all relations between human beings there is a 'third party' that intervenes. This third party often takes the form of artefacts of human activities such as money, buildings, rooms, furniture, mass communication.

The third party may be concealed. The persons involved may be unaware of its presence. But, in fact, the third party makes 'unity' possible. 'It is the third parties who unify the dyad, through the mediation of materiality' (Laing and Cooper, 1964: 111). The recognition of the inevitability of the triad may be disturbing. It reveals privacy and intimacy to be mere temporary illusions. Unification may be required by the material environment, it may be expected and planned. 'But it is always a *third party* which picks them out, through the mediation of objects' (Sartre, 1976: 114). Individuals, by necessity, live their social lives among other individuals and their relations to the others are unceasingly patterned into ternary relations constituting a 'colloid' body of social relations. Sartre writes: 'we have found that the first relation between men is the indefinite adherence of each to each'. He also calls this 'the jelly-like substance which constitutes human relations' (1976: 120).

All third parties are fragments of what Sartre calls the practico-inert field, which he describes as 'objectified praxis'. This field of inertia is made up of all existing remainders of human activities, useful as well as worthless, in the form of physical and cultural objects. Organizations and the semi-organized areas surrounding them are important ingredients in the practico-inert field. 'The field exists: in short, it is what surrounds and conditions us. I need only glance out of the window: I will be able to see cars which are men and drivers who are cars . . .' (1976: 323).

There is nothing strange about this. But the impact on social life from the forces of inertia created in the practico-inert field are often underestimated. Order is nothing but inertia. The so-called problem of social order does not need any other explanation.

Relations between men are shaped through the practico-inert field, which patterns their behaviour towards each other according to their positions in this field. Very few, if any, encounters between human beings are unaffected by these positions. This does not imply that individuals can never choose their place, but as one takes a place, one acquires new relations vis-a-vis the others.

Sartre calls these bonds between men serial relations. The connections between individuals are negatively determined through their links with objects in the practico-inert field. Even if they try, people cannot escape these bonds. Through their positions people are separated; but these separations may also be comprehended as modes of connection (1976: 221). You are separated from your neighbour by a fence or a wall, but the fence and the wall also connect you into a serial relationship. You have something in common, which also separates you.

In the series human relations are mediated through physical, social, and cultural objects. People are temporarily united around an object or an event. Their relations take place through this object. Relatives celebrating Christmas together are united by traditions and by Christmas presents. A series may comprise many people, but the relations between them are experienced in a certain order. Contacts with others are mediated through specific objects or situations. It is not primarily an experience of being one among many, but being before someone and after someone else, or above him but under her. 'As an ordering it becomes a negative principle of unity and of determining everyone's fate as Other *by every Other as Other*' (1976: 261).

The social landscape is largely what Sartre has called a practico-inert field. It is made up of objectified praxis, that is, artefacts of human activities. A nicer way to formulate this is to say that the social landscape is created by men, that it is man-made. But there is an important difference in these two modes of expression.

Saying that the social landscape is created by men somehow implies that it is intentionally designed to fit exactly the activities these men want to carry out at the same moment or in the near future. Talking about objectified praxis or artefacts, on the other hand, suggests that there may be misfits between what has been created before and the present use of that product. The product has become an artefact. The social landscape is loaded with material inertia, remnants of old activities that pattern present activities.

It is true that organizations are created by men, but as a whole, I think, they are better comprehended as objectified praxis. What happens in existing organizations is always dependent upon what is already done. They are sediments of past activities. You can only start once. This is the original sin of organizations.

Within organizations seriality is generally visible. First of all seriality is apparent in the organizational hierarchy. The bureaucratic hierarchy is a manifest series, visible and known to most people through organizational charts. It may also be evident in the way of dressing, for instance, in uniforms or other paraphernalia. Within the same hierarchical levels there may also be another less visible latent seriality. Within the same level there may be some informal ranking according to years of employment or educational qualifications. In the case of discharge from a company those with the shortest time of employment will be dismissed first. Creating seriality is fundamental to all forms of organizing.

Seriality, however, is also prevalent in relations between people outside organizations, in the semi-organized field as well as in the rest of the social landscape. People's organizational affiliations influence how they relate to each other. Kinship, citizenship, employment, membership of voluntary organizations, constitute positions in the practico-inert field which predispose encounters between people. Class is one such serial pattern (cf. Sartre, 1976: 312) built upon employment and ownership. Ethnicity is another source of seriality that has its roots in kinship relations (cf. Sartre, 1976: 267). In this way organizational affiliations have great impact on all aspects of everyday life through their seriality.

Sartre's best-known example of the series is a bus queue in the Place Saint-Germain in Paris, in front of the church (1976: 256). In a queue people arrange themselves according to their order of arrival. They constitute a series in their potential opportunity to get on the next bus. They are not waiting together; they are waiting one after the other, in different positions. The existence of the queue is also dependent upon some shared cultural values or norms among the people making up the queue, in that they accept the serial principle. Queues in the semi-organized field, however, may also be organized by the organization in question. It may supply numbered tickets to order the queue, for instance.

There are, however, competing means of seriality. If the bus is late or if the queue becomes long someone may step out of the queue and call for a taxi, that is, someone who can afford to take a taxi instead. Money cannot usually help you to get a different position in the queue at the bus stop. Seriality cannot be broken easily, but turning to monetary resources will take you into another serial structure where people are divided according to their access to these resources. Money is a form of less visible and latent seriality which potentially gives people a choice of possible organizational connections. People have many qualities constituting latent series in connection with organizations as well as semi-organized fields, such as school grades, type of education, references from previous jobs, age, sex, health status. Each quality may become the reason for placing or selecting one individual before another.

In the social landscape people seldom walk together. They pass each other, they are before or after each other, they travel at different speeds in different directions. On the way to work or going home, in the supermarket, in the street, people are separated in different kinds of series depending on the situation.

Now this is a fairly deterministic view of social life. In Sartre's social philosophy there is, however, a dialectical movement between seriality in the practico-inert field and in what he calls 'the fused group'. According to Sartre, the breaking up of the practico-inert field can only occur through the actions of the fused group. Such a group 'is being constituted by the liquidation of an inert seriality under the pressure of definite material circumstances' (1976: 361). It happens when people in a serial constellation perceive themselves as a group which 'constitutes itself on the basis of a need or common danger and defines itself by the common objective which determines its common *praxis*' (1976: 350). In this version the constitution of a fused group is a dramatic event which happens when people in a series suddenly face a common threat that abolishes their being before and after each other. People begin to act together and orient themselves towards common interests. Sartre's example in the book is the storming of the Bastille at the beginning of the French Revolution.

However, after some time, the fused group will be dissolved into a new seriality, often in the form of an organization. But during its short existence the group has changed the practico-inert field and the relations between men. It may 'produce results which belong to no system' (1976: 698). But the outbreaks of activities of fused groups are rare moments in the social world. Even if they do not necessarily occur in revolutionary situations – one may associate fused groups with wildcat strikes or various protest movements – the notion of the fused group is not sufficient to explain how human actions change the social landscape. Series are inert, but they may still be moved and changed through circumstances other than the outbreaks of fused groups. People may break out of serial relations in less dramatic ways. Even though seriality is a powerful social mechanism, series are rarely prisons. The strength of seriality is generally upheld by people's deliberate cooperation, often due to their lack of alternatives. But some people may occasionally discontinue their cooperation when they see other options. Series may be more or less attractive. Individuals are free to choose, but through seriality organizations have made some options more visible and some choices easier to make than others.

Getting off the track

For each individual the adjustment to the seriality of everyday life may be comprehended as routinization. When people join an organization or have other contacts with organizations in the semi-organized field, they usually do so to obtain some relative advantages. People accept seriality because they believe it will improve their situation. In this way individuals gradually establish a domain within the social landscape that contains several organizational affiliations covering everyday life. A person cannot go on searching and choosing for ever and the alternatives are always limited. After some time the individual will adjust to the domain and begin to feel at home. Day-to-day movements between series become routines and this routinization has a value in itself. People do not want to make new choices every morning. Giddens has expressed the importance of routinization very well. He is critical towards seeing organizational commitments as 'mutually protective contracts' (1984: 64). Even when individuals begin their organizational affiliations voluntarily, their commitments will become routines after some time and thereby lose some of their initial reasons. Routine is often reason enough. It implies at least some control of 'the world within one's reach'. As Giddens put it: 'Routinization is vital to the psychological mechanisms whereby a sense of trust or ontological security is sustained in the daily activities of social life' (1984: xxiii). Routines and habits are reinforced by serial positions. Seriality is the skeleton of routines.

Routines may be broken, however. People do not put up with something just because it is a habit. If new alternatives become visible or if things start to deteriorate individuals will eventually react. You can quit your job if you find a better one and you can change your political sympathies and join another party. The threshold for change may vary with the circumstances, and the strength of habits is great, but when an opportunity arises or when things become unbearable people will react. But how do they react?

In a couple of books Albert Hirschman has developed some concepts which have proved fruitful for this kind of analysis. The title of his first book on this topic is *Exit, Voice and Loyalty* (1970). The book is about 'responses to decline in organizations'. The question is what individuals will do when they feel dissatisfied with what they get from their organizational engagement. Basically, Hirschman's argument is that people have two possible means of reaction, either exit or voice. They may just leave the organization in silence or they may start to protest. In a later book Hirschman describes his approach as 'a *phenomenology* of involvements and disappointments' (1982: 8).

It is a way of analysing human options in the social world that tries to unite the perspectives of economics and politics. 'Exit belongs to the former realm, voice to the latter' (1970: 15). Hirschman wants to demonstrate the usefulness of economic concepts to political scientists and vice versa. His main point is that neither exit nor voice is confined to 'economic' or 'political' behaviour, but both may be equally applicable in both areas of analysis. In the extension of this argument there is also the idea that politics and markets are not contradictory poles in social life. In the social landscape both markets and politics denote processes going on between different organizations or between organizations and individuals. But Hirschman was originally an economist. He starts with a presentation of the exit option and voice is first of all regarded as a residual of exit (1970: 33). In a later book, however, Hirschman has stated that in his earlier presentation of the arguments his 'advocacy of voice was not exaggerated, but on the contrary, too timid' (1981: 214).

The notion of exit was introduced in the case of customers ceasing to buy the products of a firm when its quality deteriorates. For customers exit is the most natural reaction to dissatisfaction and it is the easiest way out as long as there are alternatives. But Hirschman also introduces exit for a situation when affiliates start to leave an organization (1970: 4). Altogether exit is a much simpler option to take.

In some situations, however, exit is not so easy. Even if Hirschman generally regards exit as less costly in terms of time and energy invested, he realizes that exit also may have its price. That is why he argues that voice is more important and common for members of organizations than for customers. Leaving the field is generally a bigger step to take for members than for customers. The choice between voice and exit is also dependent on the actual possibilities of exiting. When exit becomes difficult voice becomes more likely. Sometimes exit may even be 'wholly unavailable' (1970: 34). That is the case, for instance, according to Hirschman, in the state and in the family, in which cases voice 'is all their members normally have to work with' (1970: 17).

Compulsory membership 'by birthright may nurture voice' (1970: 97), even if it does not totally rule out the possibility of exit.

As a whole, and particularly in the first presentation of his arguments, Hirschman regards exit as the normal reaction and voice as an alternative when exit is costly or difficult or even impossible. Still, they are alternatives that can be compared and weighed against each other. Both exit and voice are means of breaking seriality and are important in comprehending the relations between organizations and individuals and how individual behaviour may change the organizational scenery. And there is probably much truth in Hirschman's observation that, whenever possible, the exit option is the most natural choice, although not always. He exaggerates the possibilities of leaving organizations and he seems to underestimate not only the costs of leaving, but in particular the opportunities to leave. He also disregards the strength of habit and routine.

In *Exit, Voice and Loyalty*, loyalty stands for an irrational affection that prevents exit from an organization: 'leaving a certain group carries a high price with it, even though no specific sanction is imposed by the group' (1970: 98). Of course, this kind of loyal behaviour is of interest in explaining why people stay in an organization even though they are becoming dissatisfied. I think, however, that another obstacle to exit is of much greater importance, namely, the lack of alternatives. Dissatisfied employees have to find other job opportunities before they can leave, which is not always easy. Not only loyalty prevents exit. Even in the case of the nation-state, I think that Hirschman has somewhat exaggerated the possibilities of exit (1981: 262). It is perhaps not impossible to leave most nation-states in the world today. But to make it possible to leave there must also be some state that is prepared to accept new citizens. For exit to be possible there must be alternatives. I believe that lack of alternatives in the practico-inert field is a better explanation than loyalty of why people stay in organizations in spite of their dissatisfaction. And it is far from certain that they will use the voice option rather than exit. There is much disappointment inside organizations that is not expressed either through exit or through voice. One concept for this is 'neglect' (cf. Rusbult et al., 1988: 601).

In what ways do exit and voice change the social landscape? When exits become plentiful they will slowly influence the growth and decline of organizations and also pave the way for new paths and passages in the organizational scenery. Exits may be seen as processes of organizational erosion. Manifestations of voice will modify organizations from within. Processes involving voice are more like the outbreaks of volcanoes or earthquakes. In the short run voice is likely to cause greater changes. Open protests or complaints are more visible and, as Hirschman says 'voice conveys more information than exit' (1981: 244) about what is wrong and how it may be taken care of. Voice demands more effort but may also give more immediate returns. Moreover, voice may, if it gains attention, turn into involvement and become a positive and constructive activity (Stryjan, 1989: 74). The notion of involvement implies active participation by individual affiliates in the shaping of the organization. It does not have to be connected with protest and dissatisfaction, however. Organizations are not only authority and control, they may also be activity and cooperation. People may become involved just for the fun of it. Involvement is not confined to particular organizational sectors, but it may be expected to be more frequent in families and voluntary organizations.

Hirschman adds that voice may be 'hazardous' (1981: 244). Voice may be transformed into positive processes of codetermination within an organization. Such changes, though, may first of all be 'in the interest of the articulate few' (1981: 244). Through voice activities some disappointments may be expressed while other grievances are left out. Some people within an organization with certain interests may be very 'voice prone' and voice or protest will thus become an end in itself. Voice may also become organized.

Exit, on the other hand, gives little information. The easiest way out is leaving without saying why. The people who stay in the organization may sometimes brand exit as an act of treachery. Those who leave are considered to be giving up too easily. In some cases exit will lead to the further deterioration of an organization, since it may lead to a negative selection of those who remain (Stryjan, 1989: 92). In this respect exit will delay or even prevent changes within an organization.

In the long run, though, exit is a strong means of change. Exits erode the foundations of organizational activities and thereby change the organizational scenery. In fact, the only way to overthrow an organization is through exit. It is not until an organization is completely deserted by all its affiliates that it is destroyed.

According to Schutz the individual is an explorer in the social landscape. Each individual investigates the world within his reach, slowly enlarging his domain and learning to master it. What may be a discovery for a single individual, however, is for most people already routine. Soon it will also become routine for the newcomer. Through exits he can start new expeditions into the surroundings. But explorations in the practico-inert field will generally only lead to finding a position in a new series. Exits do not do away with seriality but they change the social landscape into new and sometimes more comfortable series.

Both Schutz and Hirschman have stressed, in their broad phenomenological approaches to how individuals move along in the social landscape, the individual's ability to influence and change his situation. Sartre, on the other hand, has emphasized the way individuals are caught in a net of serial relations within the practico-inert field. For Sartre the only way out of this net is dramatic. The fused group will for some time liberate individuals from their serial bonds but only to leave them in a new form of seriality. The description of the fused group may be understood as a more forceful form of voice. There is, however, no concept corresponding to Hirschman's exit option in Sartre's perspective. Perhaps exit would have been uninteresting to Sartre since it does not do away with seriality. Still, it is essential to consider exits in order to understand how the organizational scenery changes through erosion. In this way it is worthwhile to combine Sartre's and Hirschman's frames of reference. Seeing seriality and inertia as the normal relation between individuals and organizations is more accurate than emphasizing loyalty. Hirschman's perspective is too voluntaristic. He overestimates the chances of moving and underestimates the power relations that prevent both exit and voice. There is much disappointment within organizations which is only expressed between colleagues and not brought into the open air. Withholding disappointments and grievances in fear of bosses and hiding certain types of behaviour or assets are common forms of individual strategy towards organizations.

Sartre's perspective, on the other hand, is too rigid. Exits do matter. And voice does not have to be as intense as Sartre has it with his notion of the fused group. Even if people are not liberated through exit or voice their general living conditions and their everyday lives may be improved considerably. But neither exit nor voice is an automatic remedy for deteriorating circumstances.

People's movements in and out of organizations must be related to the particular constellation of organizations in the terrain. Variations and changes in organizational affiliations can be described in terms of exit and voice, that is, phenomena such as labour turnover, changes in the number of members of trade unions or parties, the size of the labour force. The occurrence of exits depends on existing alternatives. An exit is more likely when there is another possible affiliation in the world within one's reach.

Exit, of course, is more relevant for describing voluntary forms of affiliation. Compulsory relations may first of all be described in terms of voice, that is in terms of protests and demands. Voice, however, also pertains to voluntary forms of affiliations, whereas exit is quite unusual in compulsory forms of affiliations, though not precluded. Exit and voice are different strategies through which individuals intentionally or unintentionally effect changes in organizational constellations.

4

Between Organizations

Individuals and organizations in the environment

Organizations cannot grow by themselves or in isolation. They feed on the environment. While organizations compete and struggle over the control of the
social landscape, they also have to rely on other organizations for support. And the interdependence of
organizations seems to increase (cf. Pfeffer and
Salancik, 1978: 43).

These chains of interdependence today stretch very
far in many directions across the social world. The same
capitalist enterprise may have different relations to
organizations such as unions, parties or nation-states in
different landscapes. The power resources of trade
unions in one social landscape cannot be understood
without relating them to the existence or non-existence
of unions in other parts of the world. The standard of
living and consumption habits of families in one part of
the world to a large extent depend on the constellation
of organizations in other parts of the world.

In the organizational scenery one will find many
forms of symbiosis between organizations. Some are
well known while others are quite unexpected, and new
forms of symbiotic relations are created now and then.
To understand the spread of the organizational scenery
in the social landscape, it is necessary to investigate how

organizations condition each other and how they interact.

Social change is not a change of systems but shifting constellations of organizations. It is not contradictions within societies or systems that are the dynamics of social change. It is the interaction and struggles between organizations within and across sectors, as well as the relations between individuals and organizations, that transform these constellations in the social landscape. Social change goes on within and between organizations and not above them.

As Perrow (1986) emphasized, organizations are not surrounded by a purely anonymous environment; a prominent aspect of the environment is other organizations. In their typology of organizations, Scott and Meyer (1983) included the influence of the institutional environment of an organization as a main variable. To proceed, however, I find it essential to think not only about the environment in terms of organizations in general. Distinguishing between the four organizational sectors, it becomes evident that we can analyse the environment of one single organization in terms of its relations with each of these four sectors.

First of all, every organization is surrounded by organizations belonging to the same sector. For at least three of the organizational sectors (excepting the nation-state), contacts with organizations within the same sector are the most frequent forms of interaction with the organizational environment. This form of interaction is generally regarded as the most natural and legitimate form of interaction. For most organizations, though, interaction with organizations from other sectors is also common and important. These relations are generally different from relations with organizations of the same sector. Altogether it is important to distinguish analytically between organizational interaction within and across sectors.

Individuals give life to organizations. Organizations cannot operate without their individual affiliates. On the other hand, individuals need organizations. Outside organizations individuals act on their own. Unorganized groups are vulnerable and generally shortlived. Still, individuals may overthrow organizations just by leaving them one by one. Often, though, to change organizations or to stop them new organizations are required.

The relationship between individuals and organizations is ambiguous. Organizations cannot exist without people. But the organization is more than the sum of the activities of its individual affiliates. Apart from its individual affiliates, an organization consists of organizational principles and tools that put it above the present individual actors. In the organization every individual is substitutable. An organization is an extra-individual artefact, but it is sterile without people.

For the individual, being part of an organization is an experience of subordination. The organization as such is always superior. Even in the least hierarchical of organizations there are several interests and wills that have to be considered. An organizational affiliation always implies yielding to the will of others, be it your teammates, your bosses, or your spouse and children. Feelings towards this subordination may vary, as well as the degree of subordination. Still, the contributions individuals make to organizations in the form of labour time, personal commitments or monetary fees, for instance, will always accumulate and thus strengthen the organizational apparatus. In an organization each individual, deliberately or not, contributes to their own subordination.

Individuals do not belong to or depend on only one organization. Monasteries are exceptional organizations today. The everyday life of most individuals is shared between several organizational affiliations and people's activities are seldom totally controlled by only one organization. Thus, an individual may be part both of the organization and of the environment at the same time. Organizations have to care about the choices and movements of individuals in the landscape.

The terrain

The encounter between organizations does not happen in a void. Organizational interaction has a background. It takes place in a particular place with its special milieu, which may influence the interaction process. The nature of the terrain is decisive in establishing the power relations between different organizations. Some organizations do better in certain kinds of terrain. The terrain has strategic relevance.

Geographically the terrain is a mixture of many kinds of botanical, geological and physical elements such as bushes, trees, mountains, lakes, rivers, marshes, deserts. In the social world the terrain surrounding organizations is a mixture of material conditions, historical traditions and social phenomena in varying combinations. Analytically the notion of the terrain, admittedly, is something of a residual category. But how could it be otherwise, when these phenomena mix in ways that cannot be summarized theoretically, and yet cannot be neglected? It makes a difference, for instance, whether the interaction between organizations takes place in a big city or in a village in the countryside.

The physical appearance of the terrain is important. For capitalist enterprises the type of activity they carry on has considerable material aspects such as the supply of raw material, machinery or geographical location. A mining company looks different from a shipping company or a real-estate firm. This has been the subject of the tradition within the theory of organizations that deals with variations in technology. Geographical positions are essential in understanding the potential of nation-states for strength and growth. Randall Collins has drawn attention to the importance of factors such as size and the quality of the land, or the difference between having neighbouring states on only one side or being surrounded by neighbouring nation-states, to understanding the processes of expansion among nation-states (1986: 187–90).

Very often, not least as jargon among social scientists, the terrain inside the borders of a nation-state is regarded as a society or a system or some other entity. But this is misleading. Even though a nation-state is defined by its territorial borders, the nation-state as an organization does not include everything that exists in this terrain. The range of control of the nation-state varies from state to state. Other kinds of organization within its territory are outside the nation-state, though. It may be regarded as a social landscape which is the coincidence of several social objects and events with different origins and nature and with little in common except being near each other at a certain point in time. This closeness does not imply a unity. Closeness is something other than similarity.

The semi-organized field of the nation-state, for instance, laws and national symbols, may create an appearance of unity across the territory, but such a unity is artificial. It can account neither for the peculiarities of the interaction between the nation-state and other organizations, nor for the development and dynamics of these organizations. There is a striking isomorphism in general organizational forms across the world which cannot primarily be related to local needs (cf. Meyer et al., 1987: 32–3). The growth and features of capitalist enterprises cannot be comprehended within their national confines. First of all their development is a consequence of changes in the technology of production and world trade which are international phenomena. The existence of families is also an international fact. Families were not created by the nation-state; they are the oldest human organizations and the changes in the structure of families have only to a limited extent been influenced by nation-states. Since voluntary associations are geographically stable, they show a greater variation across national territories. Still, voluntary organizations must first of all be regarded as cross-national phenomena. After all, political ideologies are spread across the world just like sports, for instance, and the organizational forms of voluntary organizations are remarkably similar across most nation-states.

What accounts for national traits in the interaction within and across organizational sectors is not their unity, but the very constellation of organizations from different sectors in the landscape. The individual components in this constellation do not have any inherent national characteristics, but, depending on the persistence of interaction, they may acquire certain attributes that make them different from corresponding organizations within the territories of other nation-states.

In the terrain there are social and cultural phenomena that are not directly related to the existence of organizations. Even if the organizations within a landscape display only a superficial unity, individuals in that landscape may create a unity in their domains through their common language, customs and traditions. Traditions and beliefs may occasionally have importance for understanding what goes on between organizations. Still, I would argue, culture as such has often been overestimated as an explanation of what goes on in organizations. In the long run organizations may undermine local culture and traditions in many ways, not least by the establishment of semi-organized fields.

Organizations operate and interact with other organizations and with individuals in different kinds of terrain. The content of the terrain changes across the social world. The mixture of historical, cultural and social phenomena making up the terrain changes across the social landscape; these phenomena constitute different kinds of soil for organizational growth and make certain organizational resources and tools more advantageous than others and some forms of organization more successful than others. When organizations grow they may reshape the terrain, making it more fertile and susceptible to its own operations. Thus they prepare the ground for expansion in the future.

Interaction within and across organizational sectors

For an organization to see how the land lies it is necessary to take the existence of other organizations in the terrain into consideration. Where can you find them? How are they located in the terrain and how have they adjusted to it? How many other organizations are there around and what are they actually doing? How far away are they and how fast can they move? There is a struggle between organizations about the possibilities of expansion in the social landscape. The character of the encounters between organizations varies, however, depending on whether the interaction is between organizations from the same or from different sectors.

Now, in public opinion as well as in the social sciences, there seems to be a prevalent idea that interaction between organizations should preferably occur between organizations from the same sector and that interaction between organizations from different sectors should be avoided. The most common concepts for thinking about organizational interaction are markets and politics. The idea of markets stands for the interaction between capitalist enterprises, and politics is generally conceived of in terms of interaction between political parties. Moreover, markets and politics are often regarded as two separate social institutions or principles of organization. Nothing could be more misleading.

Markets and politics are not entities clearly marked off from their surroundings in the social landscape. What is conceived of as markets or politics are particular constellations of organizations in a certain terrain. Just as meadows are particular combinations of grass, flowers and soil in a certain climate, markets are particular combinations of small enterprises and people in an open terrain. Such idyllic views are becoming quite rare nowadays, however. Markets and politics are only special forms of organizational interaction. Political competition and market competition are particular forms of struggle and conflict between organizations that may be looked upon as contained conflicts (cf. Etzioni, 1988: 216). Thus, markets and politics are not qualitatively different entities, only different constellations of organizational interaction, and as such they can be compared to each other (cf. Hirschman, 1970: 19; Lindblom, 1971: 89).

In Figure 2 I have laid out the combinations of interaction between the four sectors and given examples of interactional forms. The four cells leading diagonally from top left to bottom right represent the interactions within sectors. It is here one finds those familiar forms of interaction between organizations that correspond to the more common notions of what organizational interaction should be.

Interaction between capitalist enterprises is often described as a competition between many organizational actors in a marketplace. This is considered by many to be the most beautiful of organizational landscapes. Interaction between capitalist enterprises does not necessarily take the form of competition, however. Enterprises may

	Nation-states	Capitalist enterprises	Voluntary associations	Families
Nation-states	Wars Peace treaties Diplomacy	Law enforcement Customs Taxation	Elections Law enforcement	Child allowance Social work Taxation Hereditary succession
Capitalist enterprises	Power elites Corporatism Lobbying	Market competition Cartels	Contributions to parties Union busting	
Voluntary associations	Corporatism	Wage negotiations Strikes Codeter- mination	Political competition in elections Sporting contests	Baptism Wedding
Families	Nepotism	Ownership of companies		Rules of intermarriage Kinship systems

Figure 2   Examples of forms of interaction within and across organizational sectors

also choose to cooperate, since conflicts are costly. They can begin to negotiate the environment around them and the result may be different kinds of 'semi-formal interfirm linkages' such as interlocking directorates, joint ventures, or networks and cartels (see Pfeffer and Salancik, 1978: chap. 7).

The most widely acknowledged form of interaction between voluntary organizations is the competition between political parties before elections. This is the typical form of politics. Interaction between political parties may also take the form of negotiations in parliament. Another well-recognized form of interaction between voluntary associations is sporting contests between teams from different clubs.

The most dramatic form of interaction between nation-states is warfare. Basic interaction between nation-states is still conducted in terms of war and peace. The original form of interaction between families is intermarriage. Historically there have existed a fair number of forms and rules of intermarriage dealing with, for instance, dowries, residence, and inheritance.

These forms of organizational interaction within sectors have typically been favoured objects of research by separate disciplines within the social sciences and the humanities. Interaction between capitalist enterprises in the form of markets is the main theme of economics. Elections and the competition between political parties are at the centre of political science. The rules for intermarriage between families have been a core subject of social anthropology. Warfare and peace treaties have been a major object of historical research.

Altogether, organizational interaction within sectors, independent of which sector, has gained much attention and has been looked upon as a legitimate and somehow natural form of interaction between organizations. These forms of interaction have also stood out as ideal types in the social sciences. As such they have been widely misunderstood and have often been comprehended as independent social categories or institutions with an existence of their own, instead of being merely forms of interaction between organizations. One reason for this is the character of the interaction in terms of power resources. The organizations involved in the struggle or exchange within sectors use the same kinds of power resources. Wars are fought – by soldiers with weapons. Election campaigns are fought by way of political debate and propaganda. Market competition uses prices and products in the struggle. Traditionally at least, intermarriages have been negotiated in terms of dowries and inheritance. In the different forms of interaction within sectors the same means of power are used, even if the amount of power resources at the disposal of each actor varies. This has made the interaction more comprehensible and more like a game. In these forms of interaction it is easier to decide the balance of power between the actors, since their power resources are comparable. The parties are striving for the same goal, which makes it possible to discern who is winning and who is losing.

Interaction between organizations within sectors is less puzzling than interaction across sectors, which may even be hard to discover. Within one organizational sector the organizational entities have fully separate boundaries and are thus, in principle, clearly distinguishable. The borders of organizations from different sectors, however, often overlap. Capitalist enterprises may cross the borders of several nation-states. A trade union may organize workers in many enterprises.

Interaction between organizations from different sectors is often blurred and sometimes suspect. It is of course hard to appreciate which of these two forms of organizational interaction is most common, but I think it is safe to say that organizational interaction across sectors is a no less important phenomenon than interaction within sectors. Interaction across sectors, however, has often been neglected and looked upon as less desirable or even as reprehensible. Encounters or confrontations between organizations from different sectors are harder to conceive. It is difficult to establish rules for a struggle that is fought with disparate power resources and where the actors involved often have differing means and ends. Interaction between sectors usually means that organizations make demands on the activities of organizations in another sector in order to make them do things they otherwise would not do or to stop some of their operations. It may be a strange kind of game involving different strategies, almost like a game between a boxer and a runner.

Figure 2 also shows examples of forms of interaction across sectors: the organization in the left margin is the initiator of the interaction. For instance, some examples of interaction between a nation-state and capitalist enterprises initiated by the nation-state are customs, or state representatives on the boards of enterprises or, in a general sense, the enforcement of laws directed towards enterprises.

In the left-hand column are examples of forms of interaction directed towards the nation-state by the three other sectors. Here are some of the most common forms of interaction across sectors, which have been extensively debated and also sometimes condemned. What has sometimes been called corporatism occurs as an interaction both between capitalist enterprises and the nation-state and between voluntary organizations and the state. Lobbying is a phenomenon similar to corporatism which also belongs here. Likewise, the occasional formation of power elites is a particular form of interaction between capitalist enterprises and the nation-state. These forms of interaction have sometimes been branded as illegitimate and they are often kept secret.

Corporatism has been defined by Alan Cawson as 'a specific socio-political process in which organizations representing monopolistic functional interests engage in political exchange with state agencies over public policy outputs . . .' (1985: 8). Cawson stresses that a 'process of closure' is a distinctive feature of corporatism (1985: 9). This is why it is criticized in certain circles left out of this process.

Cawson also argues that corporatism 'can develop at different levels' (1985: 9). He distinguishes between macro-, meso- and micro-corporatism. Interaction between organizations across sectors is not a question of levels, though; it is a question of finding places to meet and entries into the other organization. Sometimes encounters may happen at 'top levels' between leaders, but the encounters may just as well be asymmetrical in hierarchical terms. For capitalist enterprises it may often be more sensible to have contacts with state representatives at lower hierarchical levels. Moreover, it is almost impossible to find comparable levels in organizations from different sectors.

Another important form of cross-sectorial interaction occurs between capitalist enterprises and trade unions. Disagreements between labour and capital about wages and conditions of work may take the form of negotiations, but may also turn into open conflicts such as strikes. This kind of interaction has often been contested by the enterprises, which have sometimes succeeded in destroying unions. On the whole it seems that capitalist enterprises prefer to interact either with other enterprises or with individuals. And when they interact with organizations from other sectors they often like it to be secret. Contacts between business leaders and government representatives are seldom announced officially; nor is capitalists' support for political parties. A recent form of interaction between enterprises and voluntary associations, sports clubs for instance, is sponsorship. This form of interaction is certainly not secret, but it is sometimes contested.

A form of interaction between families and the nation-state almost universally branded as unjust is nepotism. As a representative of the state, one is not supposed to favour one's relatives before other citizens. This form of interaction may even be regarded as criminal.

There are other forms of interaction between families and other organizational sectors, however, which are mostly regarded as legitimate, even though they too have been called into question. One example of inter-action between capitalist enterprises and families is ownership, where families may for many years retain power over one or several companies. An even more peculiar form of interaction across organizational sectors is the case of royal families, when the power to rule a nation-state has been inherited within the same family for generations.

Families are also the focus of interest of some other types of organizations. There are, for instance, voluntary organizations whose programmes aim to support both single families and the family as a form of organization. Churches, for instance, advocate the family as an important form of social organization. They also inter-vene in individual families with their message and organize activities for families rather than for indi-viduals, and they perform important functions for families, such as marriage rites. Churches may be either voluntary organizations or parts of the nation-state.

The interaction between the nation-state and families, however, does not first of all occur via the clergy or the priests. Nation-states may have many kinds of inter-action with families: allowances for the upbringing of children, compulsory education, social work for families in crisis. Families are also carefully registered and counted by the nation-state officials, since families and their incomes are an important basis for taxation. The intervention of the nation-state in families has often been branded as inappropriate.

Another form of interaction between nation-states and families occurs through legislation. But the mere existence of legislation concerning families is no true interaction. It is not until representatives or employees of the nation-state try to enforce existing laws that an interaction begins.

The two empty cells in Figure 2 indicate the diminishing

importance of families as organizations in social development, at least in Western Europe and North
America. There seem to be no important forms of
interaction initiated by families towards voluntary
organizations, or between capitalist enterprises and
families. Perhaps it would make sense to regard some
forms of consumption as interaction between enterprises and families. Generally, though, I think consumption is a matter of interaction between individuals
and enterprises in the semi-organized field. Still, families
must be reckoned with as organizations even today.

Legislation plays an important role in all cross-sectorial
interaction between the nation-state and other types of
organization, and organizations to some extent depend
upon the nation-state to support and uphold some of
their organizational forms through legislation on, for
instance, marriage or private ownership. These forms of
dependency or symbiosis have emerged gradually. The
nation-state has not created families, capitalist enterprises or voluntary associations. The nation-state is not
superimposed on other organizations. It interacts with
them in several ways and the particular forms of this
interaction are shifting. Legislation and legal procedures
are but one form of interaction.

Legislation is one of the foremost means the nation-
state has at its disposal to try to overcome the uncertainty of its environment. Laws, however, do not
constitute an organization. Legislation must be regarded
as a semi-organized field that surrounds the organizations of the nation-state. It is not only the citizens of a
particular nation-state that are expected to obey the
laws, but everybody visiting its territory. Laws are not
directed or aimed at controlling the surrounding nation-
states: they are efforts to control the landscape within
the borders of one nation-state, where there are organizations from other sectors as well as individuals.

The basis for all legislation is the particular power

resources of the nation-state, namely the monopoly of physical violence. The possession of these unique power resources does not, however, guarantee any control over the environment. Laws are often broken. And sometimes when laws are disobeyed the nation-state starts to act, but far from always and it is not certain that the actions of the nation-state will be successful. Legislation and punishment are originally designed to be applicable towards individuals (cf. Pfeffer and Salancik, 1978: 264). One cannot put organizations in prison. Legislation is a blunt instrument when directed towards organizations. Individuals in certain positions may be held responsible and even imprisoned, but the organization as such can only be punished by its own means, most often through monetary measures such as fees or fines. But, in general, organizations are harder to catch than persons.

In the semi-organized field people are anonymous. Thus, it is worth noting that people who obey the law are not identified. It is only when someone is discovered breaking the law that they are identified and treated as an individual. Inside an organization, in school, for instance, individuals have an identity all the time and their activities and performances are measured and controlled constantly, not only in a negative sense, when breaking rules, but also in a positive sense, that is, in what way and how well they accomplish their tasks. People who obey the law, however, are not registered or rewarded.

There is one important form of continual interaction between the nation-state and both enterprises and families, that is, taxation. There are mostly very detailed routines for this form of interaction. It is not easy, however, to control what happens inside other organizations. It is difficult when it comes to taxes and even harder in cases such as pollution and work environment in enterprises, or battering within families. It is much more feasible to control aspects of the semi-organized field of enterprises, for instance, the quality of goods, than to watch over events inside them, where visibility is limited.

The particular forms of nation-state authority are moulded in the interaction between the nation-state and other types of organization. Likewise, the organization of production in capitalist enterprises is shaped in interaction with organizations from other sectors, such as nation-states and trade unions. Interaction across organizational sectors is often confusing and elusive, since it involves actors with different kinds of power resources and different aims.

In the following sections I shall provide some illustrations of the processes of interaction across organizational sectors. First, I shall describe a few cases of interaction between the Swedish nation-state and other organizations within its territory. Then, I shall demonstrate how work organization in production is adjusted to particular organizational constellations in different parts of the social landscape and how supranational corporations choose their environment and the particular constellation of organizations they want to take part in. Interaction between organizations from different sectors is not confined to any society and cannot be understood as processes within systems.

The nation-state as an organization of compromises

In many respects the nation-state is the most complicated and elusive of the four organizational sectors, which can largely be explained by the particular qualities of this organizational sector. Nation-states are organizations defined by their territorial connections and boundaries. The affiliation of individuals to the nation-state is compulsory. This makes nation-states the least flexible of the organizational sectors. Geographically they are stable, and they cannot choose their citizens. Capitalist enterprises are the most flexible type of organization, and voluntary associations and families come in between, since they can either choose their members or move geographically. But the nation-state has to stick to its geographical position and to its citizens.

Nation-state authorities are specialized, but as a whole the tasks of the nation-state are of a general character. It has to address issues that come up within its territory that no other organizations want to or are able to handle. The public agencies of the nation-state will often have the most difficult tasks, the fulfilment of which is also hard to measure (cf. Meyer, 1985: 5). This, of course, does not imply that the state is the good fairy who solves all problems. It is torn between demands from other organizations and it often deals with these demands by arranging compromises, which are the effects of various forms of organizational interaction across sectors. Compromises are usually ambiguous.

Because of their relative inflexibility nation-states are often regarded as 'bureaucratic' in a derogative sense, as expressed by Michel Crozier in his book *The Bureaucratic Phenomenon*: 'the slowness, the ponderousness, the routine, the complications of procedures' (1964: 3). The nation-state has almost become the symbol of inertia. According to Crozier, the problem with state bureaucracy is that it cannot learn from its errors (1964: 187). But this explanation is too simple.

Even when people in leading positions within state agencies know what is wrong it is no easy task for them to bring about changes. Operations must continue and there are many conflicting interests involved. Moreover, differing interests may contradict each other in their analysis of errors and remedies. The organizations of the nation-state are patchworks, where new organizational forms are constructed on already existing ones.

The nation-state is organized through a 'problem-organization–problem–more organization cycle' (Meyer, 1985: 62). The elusive and inert appearance of nation-state agencies is historically rooted. Nation-states are like castles which have been rebuilt several times in different architectural styles. The problem with the state, however, is that it is not a museum, but needs to keep functioning today. It is virtually impossible to argue that the state apparatus is constructed in accordance with the interests and wishes of any particular group or class. Nicos Poulantzas remarked in his last book, criticizing earlier Marxist theories of the state, that it is 'far from self-evident that the bourgeoisie would have chosen this particular form if it had been able to tailor a State to its own requirements' (1978: 12).

Take the examples of schools and education. In Sweden employers complain that children are not disciplined enough during their education and that they do not learn the right things in school. They claim that children leaving school have 'unrealistic' expectations of job opportunities and that they are unprepared for the demands of the labour market. Certainly, if employers had tailored the educational organizations and activities they would look quite different to how they do today. On the other hand, the Swedish labour movement and the Social Democratic Party are far from satisfied with the present organization of schools and education in Sweden, despite their opportunities to carry through several educational reforms. School reforms have not been the mechanisms to abolish class differences that the Social Democrats had expected (cf. Rothstein, 1986). Changes in the organization of education have to some extent contributed to increasing equality, but the pattern of recruitment to higher education has been remarkably stable during the last twenty years. Despite political efforts to the contrary the organization of school at the end of the eighties largely reproduces previous class relations when distributing individuals to different jobs. The obstacles have been many, but most may be attributed to the inertia of the nation-state. This is not to say that it is impossible to change the activities of the nation-state but only that it needs great efforts and often the effect is much less than expected, since changes are always resisted.

The situation has been similar in most other areas of traditional state activities such as the courts, the army, communications. Roads and railways are certainly patchworks which are hard to change quickly. Group or class interests may be more clearly discernible in recently organized state agencies dealing with less traditional policy areas, but even in such cases ambiguity and elusiveness will soon blur the picture.

The ambiguity of state agencies is due not only to historical factors. The activities and legislation of the nation-state may also be incomprehensible because of the way decisions are made concerning what should be accomplished and how. Several recent authors have described the multidimensionality of these decision processes. Poulantzas writes about 'a multiplicity of diversified micro-policies' and about 'the outcome of their collision' (1978: 135). Claus Offe stresses the 'multifunctional character' of the welfare state and 'its ability to serve many conflicting ends and strategies simultaneously' (1984: 148).

In their book *The Organizational State*, Edward O. Laumann and David Knoke have investigated the making of health policy and energy policy in the United States and found that policies result 'from conflicts and contradictions among these organizational players' (1987: 6). They discovered frequent consulting and lobbying relationships, employment interchanges and communication channels between the nation-state and interest groups, creating 'the inseparably intertwined institutions that constitute the modern state' (1987:

381). The problem with their approach, however, is that they have concentrated their work so much on these 'policy domains' as 'subsystems' that they have mixed up the interaction processes and the organizations involved. Even though interaction across organizational sectors is complex it must be separated from the organizations involved. It is complicated because the interacting organizations are from different organizational sectors, which means that the incorporation of one organization into the other is less feasible; the choice between 'markets and hierarchies' is harder to accomplish and thus less likely to occur across organizational sectors.

Decisionmaking on state policies is a continuous process of interaction between the nation-state and organizations from other sectors. This interaction occurs in many parts of the terrain and it changes character according to shifting power resources and varying elements of the terrain. It is a protracted process and it is seldom that any winners or losers can be selected. There is a mixture of forms of cross-sectorial interaction and various principles of decisionmaking. Negotiations between corporate actors are mixed with voting in representative bodies. It is often impossible to distinguish between the creation and the implementation of public policy (cf. Rothstein, 1987: 307). This interaction sometimes becomes garbage-can decision processes, where problems, solutions and choice opportunities are mixed up and where participants come and go and the outcome is unpredictable (Cohen et al., 1982: 26–7). Garbage-can decision processes have first of all been discovered within nation-states, and it might be tempting to regard the nation-state as a huge garbage can, but that would be going too far.

To understand the rationale behind decisions and policies it is mostly necessary to reconstruct long chains of decisionmaking involving compromises and deals between several organizations, the results of which may best be described as nobody's policy and for which no party wants to take the full responsibility.

A recent example of a big policy issue that was finally settled as a compromise was the struggle over wage-earners' funds. In the mid-seventies the Swedish trade union federation of blue-collar workers (LO) launched a proposal for profitsharing among employees and shareholders in capitalist enterprises. Through successive transfers of certain portions of annual company profits to funds controlled by union representatives, employees would gradually gain a substantial power position in these companies (see Himmelstrand et al., 1981). This quite far-reaching proposal aroused furious protests and large demonstrations among capitalists as well as small employers. The idea of wage-earners' funds was most ardently supported by the trade unions, whereas the Social Democratic Party was hesitant. When the question of wage-earners' funds was finally made an issue at the 1982 elections, the Party, in fear of protests from employers, came to a compromise with the central union organization. After the election, which was a success for the Social Democrats, an arrangement with regional funds was established. These funds get limited proportions of company profits which they invest in the stock market, and their aim is not to gain influence in or control of the companies. They administer their capital more or less like any other financial enterprise. This compromise does not satisfy any of the original demands from unions, and the funds are still contested by employers. It was a process of interaction between several types of organization that in the end produced 'results which belong to no system (not to those which are in conflict, nor to a new one)' (Sartre, 1976: 698).

Compromises are reached when no party expects to be able to win. They are ways of not losing everything. Compromises are strategic decisions and thus intentional. The intentions may be hard for an outsider to discover, however, since the result is something that nobody wanted from the beginning. In this respect compromises are unintended consequences occurring when an organization encounters resistance which it cannot overcome. The nation-state is founded on compromises. What above all unites the citizens of a nation-state is their living closely together in a limited territory. Their interests may vary, however. Thus, in order to get along, they need an organization to settle or at least suspend their conflicts. The nation-state does this through the organization of compromises.

Even if a branch of the nation-state is not a compromise from the start, it may meet with resistance and acquire the character of a compromise after some time. This is the case of the state employment exchange in Sweden, which pays out unemployment benefit during periods of unemployment.

The state monopoly of employment exchange was established at the end of the forties as an initiative by the trade unions and the Social Democratic Party. The aim was to construct an antibureaucratic organization in the service of the working class. Many trade union activists were employed to avoid clashes between educated bureaucrats and workers. Interaction with employers was built into the organization at several hierarchical levels. The activities of the employment exchange became more ambitious during the sixties and the beginning of the seventies under pressure from the unions. Those in search of jobs were to have as much information as possible about job opportunities on the labour market and the ambition was to help them to find jobs as far as possible in line with their wishes and qualifications. There was also legislation making it compulsory for employers to report all vacancies to the employment exchange (see Ahrne, 1989: 99–102).

Employers, however, have had extensive opportunities to resist offensive strategies from the employment exchange and also to use it for their own purposes. Unions and politicians have had a stronger hold on the employment exchange organization at top levels, whereas employers have been better able to use their particular power resources at local levels of the organization. Enterprises have always complained that they do not get the right kind of people from the labour exchange. They do not want too many people applying for their vacancies, either. In exchange for the compulsory reporting of vacancies, the employers have demanded that the staff of the employment exchange should select two or three suitable candidates for each job, but have held firmly on to the right to make the final decision on whom to employ. During the eighties the routine of the employment exchange has changed, so that the staff now have to start by finding suitable people for the vacancies they have, instead of first looking for suitable jobs for the unemployed. The officials of the employment exchange have also become more closely tied to particular enterprises. They now do some of the work of the personnel departments of the companies. Through their power position as employers, the companies have been able to change the content of the activities of the employment exchange quite substantially. Still, one cannot argue that the employment exchange merely serves the interests of the employers. Its routines and practices have become compromises. It is an illustration of how nation-state organizations are shaped in constant interaction with other organizational sectors according to their particular power resources.

The outcome of such processes within the nation-state to a large extent depends on their position in the terrain. The employment exchange has been established in an exposed terrain where its development has been much influenced by its closeness to employers. As a contrast to this development, the sickness insurance organization may be mentioned. It has been established in a more protected terrain further away from the influences of employers. This is one of the reasons why the organizations of the labour movement have been more successful in keeping the sickness insurance organization working in their interest than in the case of the state labour exchange. The sickness insurance programme does not need the cooperation of the employers in the same way, and employers have no representation within this branch of the nation-state. However, when it comes to the rehabilitation of sick people and finding new jobs for them, the sickness insurance organization is in the same position as the labour exchange in its need to interact with enterprises. It is more feasible to accomplish welfare state arrangements within the confines of the nation-state, such as sickness insurance or pensions, than to make arrangements that are exposed to resistance from other organizations. Here one discovers the organizational limits of the welfare state to gain control in the social landscape.

The organizational limits of the welfare state

When demands on the nation-state concern certain aspects of what other organizations do, it is impractical to include the whole organization within the confines of the nation-state. Some of the strongest demands on the welfare state today have this character, for instance demands for improved work environments, creating jobs for disabled people, or preventing environmental pollution. To try to fulfil this kind of demand the most common strategy for the nation-state is to extend its semi-organized field through legislation or other measures. The semi-organized field, however, implies a considerably lower degree of control than having the activities within the organization itself. The ability to control the environment through a semi-organized field depends on how the qualities of the nation-state are adjusted to the terrain in comparison with the objects of control. Some things are easier to control than others, depending upon technology, visibility, size, etc.

Apart from legislation, the nation-state has other means at its disposal to try to influence the environment, such as propaganda and information. The effectiveness of these means, however, is often limited. The nation-state, moreover, can use fiscal means to encourage certain kinds of behaviour among surrounding individuals and organizations and prevent others. The design of tax regulations is a way of trying to influence what happens in the environment, the effects of which vary widely. At times the nation-state can encourage certain activities through direct subsidies, for instance, child allowances to families or subsidies for enterprises establishing production in certain regions.

Still, the primary means of semi-organizing by the nation-state is legislation. In principle the power of legislation rests upon the nation-states' right to stop people from doing certain things by the use of violence or to punish them for what they have done, and the access to resources to do this, namely the police and the military. In practice, however, the value of these power resources is sometimes limited. This is the case when legislation is directed towards other types of organization, particularly capitalist enterprises. Many of the demands to increase the activities and the control of the welfare state concern what goes on inside companies. These demands are not so easily fulfilled. Enterprises have many ways of resisting control. The problems of enforcing the law on work environment, for instance, may be understood in terms of organizational interaction across sectors. It is a confrontation between different kinds of power resources involving different organizational strategies.

The nation-state is tied to its territory and it is geographically divided into smaller units. Its borders are long and require power resources to be spread out in order to watch them all. The nation-state is immobile, and slow, but it is also strong. The nation-state seldom gives up.

Compared to the nation-state, capitalist enterprises are mobile and flexible. If they are attacked they can move their operations and they can largely choose where to locate themselves. They will do what is profitable or else they will just go out of business. Capitalist enterprises can concentrate their own resources, and they usually have a better knowledge of the relevant terrain.

The Swedish nation-state does not mobilize its army or its police force to enforce the Work Environment Act in factories or in restaurants. There is a special agency for this purpose, the Labour Inspectorate. It is the job of the inspectors to look after the work environment in all the places of work in their district. For practical reasons the inspectors usually announce their visits to a company in advance. The inspectors are not armed when they go on their visits and they usually go alone. The power resources of the inspectors are limited and their disadvantageous position when they visit a factory is typical of the conditions of the nation-state in these forms of interaction with capitalist enterprises.

Even though the inspector has a general knowledge of conditions of work and technology, in each particular place of work he has to depend on information from managers with higher education and status than himself, and often he cannot even find his way through the buildings and the workshops. He is left at the mercy of the company, and the strategy of the inspectors is generally very cautious, mostly trying to influence the companies by giving information about risks. It is exceptional for legal measures to be taken (Lundberg, 1982). The situation of officials from the regional boards for environmental protection controlling pollution from factories is similar (see Ahrne, 1989: 139).

Enterprises are specialists in their own field of production and activity and it is important for them to mobilize resources to resist measures from the state. Building inspectors controlling the planning and construction of new houses and offices complain that they have no means of following up the development of new construction material and technology, which makes their position difficult. Even though the nation-state makes the laws, enterprises often have experts who know the laws better than the local state administrators.

The slowness of the nation-state is another drawback in its interaction with capitalist enterprises. There are many things the state has to do and there are many interests to cater for. Decisions take a long time. Builders, who usually want their building permits more quickly than the normal three or four weeks, may very well get their permits in a couple of days, if they threaten to dismiss workers. Of course, this diminishes the ability of the building authorities to control the quality of new houses.

Legal procedures are slow. That is why towns often deliberately refrain from using their right to expropriate land for large construction projects. The towns need the cooperation of the building firms, but if projects are delayed, the building firms may pull out, since time costs money. The municipality may become involved in an exchange of land, to speed up the process, and offer some of its own land in exchange for the site it needs for a particular project instead of acquiring it through legal procedures.

In their interaction the nation-state (including local authorities) and capitalist enterprises operate under different restrictions and with different kinds of power resources. In interaction between enterprises there is a natural means of equivalency, namely money, which

smooths the interaction. In interaction across organizational sectors there is no such given means of
equivalency. That is why negotiations between organizations from different organizational sectors often turn
into a primitive barter. When legislation is ineffective
the nation-state authorities will have to negotiate things
that are not negotiable.

Building firms usually make plans which overstep the
restrictions on several issues such as number of flats,
size of playgrounds, access to lifts. Trying to uphold at
least some of the regulations, the officials will have to
negotiate different kinds of violations against each
other: if the firm builds the prescribed number of flats it
will be allowed to make smaller playgrounds, etc. In the
case of the state labour exchange there is a law that can
force employers to employ handicapped people under
certain circumstances. This law has never been applied,
however. Instead, the officials of the labour exchange
sometimes exchange handicapped people with employers. If the company employs a disabled person the
labour exchange may in return take responsibility for an
employee whom the employer wants to get rid of
(Ahrne, 1989: 150-1).

The movements and adaptations of capitalist enterprises

The purpose of the two previous sections has not been
to demonstrate that capitalist enterprises are the most
powerful of organizations. They cannot accomplish all
they want. The point is that they have different kinds of
power resources from organizations from other sectors,
so that they have strategic advantages in certain
situations. Generally, when analysing interaction
between organizations from different sectors, one has
to be careful in comparing their power resources. The
strength of various kinds of power resources depends on

their particular form and use in the terrain. One cannot estimate the value of different kinds of power resources without putting them in a context.

In this section I shall discuss how the organization of production varies in different kinds of terrain because of shifting organizational constellations. Like all organizations, capitalist enterprises have to adjust to the circumstances, but unlike nation-states and voluntary associations they can choose their environment and move to a more favourable part of the social landscape where their particular power resources will be more useful.

Electrolux is a Swedish-owned corporation which has 147,000 employees in 500 subsidiary companies in 50 countries. It specializes in the manufacture of white goods – washing machines, refrigerators and so on. During the last ten years it has bought a number of companies in this line of business. All the subsidiaries of Electrolux have a common detailed accounting system, which is computerized. On the 16th of every month the headquarters in Stockholm will check the closing accounts of all the subsidiaries via computer terminals. The demands on profits are equally high in all subsidiaries, as are the demands on the quality of the products. Electrolux, however, does not have a common policy or any common regulations on how to organize production, or a common policy towards trade unions. It is up to individual subsidiaries to find their own solutions to organizational problems.

The headquarters of Electrolux is still located in Sweden, but it is uncertain whether production will remain within this terrain. According to the President of Electrolux, Sweden has a 'very bad industrial climate'. The main reason for this is the organization of the nation-state. The two big problems for Electrolux in Sweden are high labour turnover and a high rate of absence through sickness. The state policy of low unemployment and liberal sickness benefits gives people the chance to choose. Measures taken by the nation-state have made it easier for individuals to move around in the terrain between different organizations. In such a situation capitalist enterprises have no means of forcing people to come to work. In this respect their power resources are limited.

In northeastern England the organizational constellation is different. Unemployment is high. In an Electrolux subsidiary in Spennymoor the labour turnover is very low, as is absence through sickness. In this factory the problem is rather that people come to work when they are ill, since they cannot afford to stay at home. These differences affect the organization of labour. To keep people in the work force, Electrolux in Sweden has to improve the work environment and make jobs more stimulating by introducing various forms of job enrichment, whereas in the factory in Spennymoor there is increasing division of the organization of work. In the factory in Sweden production is to a large extent computerized, which is not the case in the subsidiary in England.

For the trade unions at Electrolux in Sweden one long-term strategy is to strengthen unions in other Electrolux factories throughout the world. The only way to keep production in Sweden is to try to create similar conditions for workers in other Electrolux factories. This is a difficult task and it seems that the unions at Electrolux in Spennymoor have limited interest in cooperation with the unions in Sweden to try to save the jobs there (Barkman, 1989).

In a very illuminating analysis the American sociologist Michael Burawoy discusses the variation of what he calls 'factory regimes' according to relations between capitalist enterprises and nation-states. In his book *The Politics of Production* he presents a comparative historical perspective on the development of changing factory regimes. According to Burawoy 'each particular factory regime is the product of general forces operating at a societal or global level' (1985: 18). Early capitalist production took place under what may be called 'market despotism' with hardly any interference from the nation-state. Burawoy, however, underlines that this was an exceptional situation (1985: 14). Generally speaking, the relations of production in individual capitalist enterprises have been formed in interaction between nation-states and enterprises. Burawoy also takes the strength of trade unions into consideration (1985: 67, 136).

Burawoy distinguishes between four 'national configurations of state regulation of factory regimes' (1985: 138). They differ with respect to the extent of the intervention of the state in the reproduction of labour power and in direct state regulation of the labour process. The organization of production in factories in Japan and Sweden represents opposite poles. In Swedish factories state intervention is high, whereas it is low in Japanese factories. The two other cases are England and the United States.

Burawoy compares two similar factories in these latter countries. Basically, he finds that the workers in the English factory had 'more control over the labour process, and therefore more bargaining power with management' (1985: 132). The struggle over wages went on continually on the shop floor through occasional short strikes. In the American factory these relations were inscribed in stable rules. These differences must be comprehended in terms of the varying constellations among enterprises, trade unions and the nation-state. In the English case, for instance, the pattern of unionization fosters militancy on the shop floor, whereas in the United States collective bargains are legally binding (1985: 137). Moreover, in the United States workers are more dependent on enterprises for social benefits through arrangement of internal labour markets, which creates stability in the process of production. In England these social benefits are delivered by the state, which makes workers less dependent on the company.

Comparing differences in the organization of production in enterprises in Japan and the United States it is important to look at their relations to individuals, whose ability to move around in the landscape will influence the strategy of employers. Many of the paternalistic features of enterprises in Japan can be explained by the shortage of skilled labour that the industry faced at the beginning of this century. Paternalistic arrangements in the enterprise were efforts to tie employees to one enterprise in order to reduce turnover (Littler, 1982: 152). In the United States the industry also had high turnover, but at the same time more people were constantly arriving in the terrain. Enterprises adjusted to this situation by 'structuring work organization around a mobile, shifting immigrant labour force' (Littler, 1982: 185). This was one of the origins of Taylorism.

As I have stressed in the previous section there are limits to the possible interventions of the nation-state in the organization of capitalist enterprises. When things go too far, when the 'climate' becomes too rough, enterprises can try to move to a more favourable location in the social landscape. Burawoy has also underlined this tendency, which has been facilitated by recent technological developments (1985: 263).

Corporations do not only move from a location within the territory of one nation-state to another; they become not just multinational but also supranational. Through being mobile between the territories of several nation-states, large corporations may also become less vulnerable to nation-state intervention in general.

In August 1987 the Swedish company ASEA announced its merger with the Swiss electrical engineering group Brown Boveri, which led to the creation of one of the largest corporations in this line of business in the world. The Swedish government and the trade unions were informed two days in advance. The unions in Sweden were not opposed to the plans until it was decided that the headquarters of the new corporation was to be located in Zurich.

Through the location of the headquarters in Switzerland the trade unions in Sweden lost their legal rights to have negotiations with the management about the most strategic decisions at the top level. Their influence has been curtailed and since the merger they may only take part in decisions on the operations of the section of ABB that remains in Sweden (Elvander, 1989: 82–3).

This development has caused much concern among trade unions in several countries and efforts have been made to increase cooperation between unions in order not to lose influence in supranational corporations. The strategy among corporations, however, has been to refuse to make any transnational agreements involving unions from different countries. They want contacts with the unions to be restricted to subsidiaries in different countries according to national legislation. With national legislation, however, unions will have difficulty in gaining access to relevant information about the corporation as a whole. It is not only that these corporations are located in many nation-states and move resources between them according to where they find the terrain most suitable. It is even more important that supranational corporations, when ownership becomes international, can escape the changing legislation of all the nation-states involved, since the central power of the corporation is not located in any one country. The conclusion reached by the trade unions in Sweden after the merger between ASEA and Brown Boveri was that the power of the corporation had not been transferred from Sweden to Switzerland. Instead 'the result is that both countries involved lose national control' (Elvander, 1989: 84).

Interaction between organizations from different sectors is decisive in determining the particular form or design of agencies of the nation-state as well as of branches or subsidiaries of capitalist enterprises. Organizations from different sectors interact in a different way from organizations within the same sector. Organizations from different sectors are not striving for the same goals, so they are not competing with each other. Instead they make demands on each other. Both trade unions and enterprises make demands on the nation-state, the nation-state makes demands on enterprises and unions, and unions also make demands on enterprises, etc. Organizations from different sectors interact to try to influence or force the other organizations to do things they would not otherwise do, or prevent them from doing certain things. This does not happen in interaction within the same sector.

Capitalist enterprises have several ways of escaping demands. For the nation-state it can be difficult to control the operations of enterprises, and enterprises can move their activities across nation-states and away from unions. But enterprises also have to adjust their activities to fulfil some of the demands of other kinds of organizations in order to carry on. The strength of demands from other organizations depends on the constellation of organizations in a particular location and their ability to use their power resources.

The shaping of the organization of the manufacture of the same product in the same corporation may vary considerably in different parts of the social landscape due to the particular organizational configuration there. The organizational actors are the same but their combination and strength vary. The four factory regimes that Burawoy distinguished are the effects of different constellations of organizations across sectors, which overlap and intermingle in various combinations.

The linking of affiliations in everyday life

Individual identities are moulded and constructed within varying constellations of organizational affiliations in everyday life. Individuals are both inside and outside organizations. People split their everyday lives between affiliations to organizations in different sectors. They also spend much time in the semi-organized fields, in the supermarket, in the bus or in front of the TV. Everyday life is characterized by routine and seriality, sometimes broken by exits or protests. In the course of a day people move in and out of anonymity in semi-organized fields to various organizational identities. The border between anonymity and identity is sharp in modern social life. Anonymity resides between organizations.

To be affiliated to an organization means to be registered there and to be identified. One's actions as an affiliate are watched, measured and judged. One has commitments but also rights. In the social sciences the two most studied forms of organizational affiliations are probably employment and kinship. They are also the two most frequent and important forms of affiliation in everyday life. Still, in many respects other forms of affiliation may be just as important, such as ownership, membership of voluntary associations or citizenship. These forms of association, though, are more often more ambiguous and less well understood.

Citizenship is a rather obscure form of organizational affiliation. Since it is compulsory, it is fundamental in certain respects. But people do not usually act as citizens every day or every week. In fact, citizenship has limited importance in everyday life, except for children attending compulsory school. Normally, as a citizen one spends most of one's time outside the bureaucracy of the nation-state. Citizenship mostly pertains to situations where the stability of everyday life is threatened by, for instance, unemployment, illness, environmental pollution or perhaps by political events of some kind.

Citizenship can partly be comprehended in terms of 'specific sets of rights and the social institutions through which such rights are exercised' (Barbalet, 1988: 6). In his well-known article 'Citizenship and social class' (1965), the English sociologist Thomas H. Marshall distinguished three elements of citizenship: civil rights, political rights and social rights. Each of these has 'different institutional bases, and in significant respects different histories' (Barbalet, 1988: 6). Among these social citizenship developed last and, moreover, it is not fully developed. Citizenship implies equal status among all those who are full members of a nation-state. Included in social rights are the rights to education, social benefits and certain social services. Social citizenship rights have been established as counteracting forces in relation to the development of capitalist production; as Marshall expressed it, 'it is clear that in the twentieth century, citizenship and the capitalist class system have been at war' (1965: 93). Social rights have been less fully developed than equality before the law, or political participation, which may be comprehended in terms of the organizational limits of the welfare state. The growth of social rights is 'achieved through a compromise which is not dictated by logic' (Marshall, 1965: 134). They have been founded through long decision processes where the original demands have encountered resistance. They have been established in interaction between several organizational sectors and their design is determined by this interaction.

This is one reason why social rights may seem amorphous (cf. Barbalet, 1988: 70). They are not always coherent. Citizenship rights increase equality, but for an individual citizen to make use of his rights can still be confusing. The organizational design of a particular right is rarely straightforward. It is a product of many organizational influences.

Citizenship is a matter between individuals and the nation-state. Neither families nor any other organizations are citizens. People make use of their citizenship rights individually, one by one. Even though social rights have been gained collectively through organized struggles, each individual is in an exposed position when turning to the nation-state to claim his rights. Nobody will press them upon him. Increased social rights often come with 'an extension of state influence and control' (Lipsky, 1980: 4). The first form of organizational control of affiliates is identification. To gain access to their social rights citizens have to prove their identity. In Sweden publicly employed doctors have to ask patients for their identity cards even when examining them in their homes. Even though social benefits of various kinds are rights, to gain access to your rights you have to prove your eligibility, you may be exposed to control. This is not usually a problem, yet people's experiences of contacts with nation-state agencies are often ambiguous. Complications are not unusual due to the slowness and the ponderousness of the state.

To make use of citizenship rights is to be registered, watched, measured, and judged just as in all forms of organizational participation. But citizens are not only watched and judged according to their actual performance, as at school, for instance. In the case of social rights, citizens are categorized according to their organizational affiliations: their positions and past performance in their jobs, their family affairs, their membership of any unions or other voluntary organizations. Seriality is the basis of the bureaucratic identity of individuals. The conglomeration of the nation-state is reflected in its description of its citizens. In their contacts with the bureaucracy of the state people are received as individuals by nice, gentle officials, but they are treated as socially constructed cases.

Swedish citizens are entitled to pensions after the age of 65. But the size of the pension is determined by past income and number of years of employment. The kinds of job people may ask for at the employment exchange are determined by their previous jobs and their level of education. The right to sickness insurance is determined not only by the illness but also by the kind of work one has and by how much time one has worked before. The right to get a flat from the local housing authorities is determined by one's family situation. For the bureaucracy of the nation-state a citizen is a social construction of his relevant organizational affiliations.

It is hard for individuals to escape their social identity. Getting new citizenship of another nation-state takes many years, if it is at all possible. Exits from the nation-state take time, and voice too is hazardous in individual cases. Another form of exit is to turn to other organizations for help instead of making use of citizenship rights. An alternative individual strategy towards the nation-state is withdrawal.

Marshall distinguishes between citizenship and class. Class, however, is an ambiguous concept in terms of organizational affiliations. Class positions may be understood as descriptions of important aspects of various kinds of organizational affiliation, in particular, relations of power within organizations. People having similar positions may be regarded as belonging to the same class, even though they are affiliated to different kinds of organization.

In a general sense, though, Marshall was right to contrast citizenship with class, since class may comprise all kinds of organizational affiliations except citizenship. There is no class model that includes citizenship as an aspect of class. The two forms of organizational affiliation that are most relevant for describing class positions are ownership and employment. The bourgeoisie is usually defined through ownership of capital. The working class consists of employees in capitalist enterprises and in nation-states. Intermediate classes with contradictory class positions are employees with privileged positions in hierarchical terms within different types of organization. The petty bourgeoisie, that is, peasants and artisans, is to a large extent constituted in kinship terms. When it comes to class organizations the relevant aspect is membership of voluntary associations such as trade unions or labour parties. Class models or class maps, therefore, may be composed of elements from all kinds of organizational affiliations except citizenship.

The class position of an individual is determined by one or more aspects of his organizational affiliations. Generally, a class position is supposed to delineate conditions that are important for understanding the living conditions and societal outlook of individuals as members of a certain class. And indeed this is often the case. Still, an individual's class position does not say everything about his everyday life. Participation in other forms of organized activities as well as in the semi-organized field also affect individual values and identities. For many people, particularly women, the class position of their spouse is just as important as their own class position in forming their social consciousness. In an empirical analysis of temporality and class, the conclusion is: 'the effectivity of the individual experiences that are constitutive of class depends upon the historical context within which those experiences occur' (Wright and Shin, 1988: 83). The organizational constellations in people's everyday lives often contain contradictory messages which are difficult to integrate into a consistent pattern of values. People learn how to handle such contradictions on a practical level, as practical consciousness, even though the situation can cause problems in terms of the discursive consciousness (cf. Giddens, 1984). Shifting organizational constellations imply shifting routines of everyday life which also affect the social identity and outlook.

5

Summary: Organized Actors, Unorganized Organizations

Just as there is only one nature on earth, there is only one society today. It seems no longer meaningful or possible to conceive of the social world as divided into separate societies or systems covering the world side by side. People's everyday lives may just as well be determined by events happening on the other side of the globe as by what takes place on the other side of the street. People's connections to other individuals or organizations far away may be more important than their relations with their neighbours. The connections between geographical and social units have been dissolved, which has only increased the importance of considering the geographical and spatial aspects of social life. Technological innovations, recessions, booms, stock exchange rates as well as trademarks, sports, fashion, music, literature, films, TV programmes, news, are all phenomena that are rapidly spreading around the social world mediated via organizations breaking the boundaries of systems or societies. These processes affect most people, albeit far from equally, for better or for worse.

Yet much recent theorizing in the social sciences has focused on relations and exchanges between individual actors and systems or structures. Jürgen Habermas' elaboration of the relationship between communicative action, lifeworld and system as well as Anthony Giddens' theory of structuration are examples of this trend. I have argued, however, that there are two flaws in this line of theorizing. First, it tends to make the relations between individuals and society unnecessarily abstract and elusive. Second, the idea of systems or structures as social entities with an existence of their own is irrelevant to social analysis today. It hides more than it discloses in terms of relations between organizations that operate on a global scale. I suggest instead that we should focus on the relations between individual actors and organizations on one hand, and the relations between different kinds of organizations, on the other. Below I shall summarize the arguments in this outline of an organizational theory of society.

Individuals in organizations

People do not belong to systems or structures but are affiliated to various organizations. Organizational affiliations are the bonds that connect individuals with society and they are decisive in forming the social position of individuals and in establishing social control.

For organizations individual affiliations are crucial. Affiliation is the basic component of organizing. To each individual, to be affiliated to an organization means having commitments as well as rights. Affiliation gives permanence to the organization; it implies a promise to return. Without affiliations an organization would be merely a gathering of people.

Affiliation and organization are a way of coordinating individual actions which makes the organization into an extraindividual unit. Coordination also implies a division of labour and some forms of authority. Once an organization is constituted it becomes independent of its individual affiliates and they become interchangeable. Individuals give life to organizations but organizations are not dependent on particular individual actors. They may come and go.

In contrast, a group of friends is not an organization. Perhaps they meet regularly for some activities, but friends are not interchangeable. One cannot recruit new friends just like that. Moreover, friends do not control each other nor do they have authority over each other.

Organizational affiliation is a formal category and very clear-cut. One is either an affiliate of a particular organization or not. As an affiliate one is registered and identified. One's presence in the organization is documented. One's performance is registered and either punished or rewarded. The control inside organizations is a connection of identified individuals to a certain place at a certain time. Moreover, the organizational control over individual affiliates is cumulative. Performance and presence are registered and accumulated for days, weeks and years.

One can discern four basic types of individual affiliation to organizations: membership, ownership, kinship and citizenship. They correspond to four organizational sectors: voluntary associations, enterprises, families, and nation-states. Then there is a fifth type of affiliation, since it does not include the same kind of rights, that is, employment. Employment pertains to all four organizational sectors. This definiton of what organizations are may be considered as an extended notion of organization which also includes what are sometimes regarded as social institutions. When looked at from the point of view of individual affiliations this extended definition becomes obvious, however.

Organizations are not primarily repressive. First of all they give people opportunities and provide resources for important activities. To be organized gives strength, security and protection. Organizations are the settings for routines and regularity.

Organizational affiliations also give identities to

individuals, such as family name, occupational title, citizenship, political colour. People are often referred to in terms of their organizational affiliation as coming from a certain family, being of a certain nationality, belonging to a certain club, or being employed by a certain company. To be organized is to belong somewhere and to be recognized. Outside organizations, in the semi-organized field, there is anonymity.

In everyday life people have many relations with organizations without being among their affiliates. Travelling on a bus to work, shopping in the supermarket, going to the theatre or listening to a political speech implies taking part in the semi-organized field of various types of organization. Here people are generally not identified. They are not known according to their past performance and they do not have to be at a certain place at a certain time unless they want to. As customers, spectators, or passengers, people have no commitments. Perhaps the staff at the grocer's recognize your face, but they probably don't know your name. For practical reasons a subscriber to a newspaper has to state his name and address, but this is hardly an identification and it entails no control. Time spent in the semi-organized field is generally described as leisure time, or free time.

The case is not, as has been argued, that the modern social world generally means increasing anonymity. What is happening is that the zone between recorded identities in organizations and the anonymity of the semi-organized field has diminished. Informal groups and small communities have lost much of their importance. These gatherings are more dependent on the contributions and participation of particular individuals, who are not substitutable. Informal groups are vulnerable to change when people's everyday lives become disconnected and when people in their daily activities pass each other in anonymity in buses or cars between their organizational commitments or on holidays in the semi-organized field along the beaches of the world.

Organizations operate in different kinds of terrain. They are part of a social landscape, where there is a mutual adaptation among various elements that have been brought together casually. Their closeness in the landscape does not make them into units, however.

For individuals trying to situate themselves in the social landscape the organizations are already there as objectified praxis from the past activities of other people. The social landscape is a practico-inert field made out of remnants of human efforts. In this landscape individuals try to establish a domain of their own. The domain is a manipulatory area which the individual can control through his bodily movements. The routines of everyday life are to a large extent set up within organizations. During the day people move between their homes and their jobs, sometimes also taking part in the activities of voluntary associations. In the breaks between organizational sojourns they can spend their free time in the semi-organized fields within their reach.

Everyday life consists of a complicated network of relations and connections between people and organizations. Routines are stable and inert. They are repeated every day. Now and then, however, people change their organizational affiliations and their everyday routines by exiting from organizations. When this happens there are usually alternatives available in the world within reach. The individual's range of choices in the social landscape is usually narrow. In the long run, however, individual exits from organizations can erode the organizational scenery. Individual choices and actions do change the social landscape.

The opportunities and preconditions for moving between organizations vary with organizational sector. In fact, what distinguishes the four organizational sectors is their particular connections to individual affiliates. Their differences are constituted by their different bonds to individuals and everyday life. The four sectors can be distinguished in terms of compulsory or voluntary affiliations and in terms of their mobility or stability.

The affiliation to capitalist enterprises is voluntary, and they are spatially mobile. In capitalist enterprises both affiliation and location can change considerably and rapidly. Nation-states, on the other hand, are tied to their affiliates as well as to their spatial location. It is difficult for people to change citizenship and it is almost impossible for the nation-state to get rid of its affiliates. Capitalist enterprises are more flexible as organizations than nation-states.

Voluntary associations are founded on members coming from the same place or district, which makes such organizations spatially stable, even if their membership is voluntary. For its activities such an organization has to stick to its particular location. Families, on the other hand, are mobile. Family organizations are kept together through kinship, which is compulsory. The bonds between parents and children are there even when they live far apart.

In this way organizations from different sectors have varying foundations in people's everyday lives. Capitalist enterprises may disappear, whereas the nation-state is always there. People may change their affiliations to political parties or sports clubs, but they can never escape their kinship.

These preconditions for relations to affiliates and to the geographical location largely affect the power resources and strategies available to organizations from different sectors.

Unorganized organizations

Social life must be comprehended and analysed on a global scale; the bulk of world society consists of organizations which have long since broken all societal or systemic boundaries. Organizations operating in the same part of the social landscape are highly dependent for their operations on connections with other organizations of the same kind which are located far away in several directions. Organizations are interdependent, but organizations that operate close to each other are not necessarily those that have the strongest interdependency. The various relations of interdependence pertaining to organizations located in the same place do not coincide in a system. Some researchers have realized the problematic nature of the notion of systems, and have started to talk about open systems instead. But how open can systems become before they cease to exist? I maintain that, to understand organizational interdependencies and strategies on a global scale, it is necessary to investigate what goes on between organizations. This interaction, however, is not organized.

In doing this, it is essential to distinguish between organizations from separate sectors. Organizations from the same sector have many fundamental qualities in common. They are always more like other organizations from the same sector than they are similar to organizations from other sectors, even if they operate in the same location. And all four organizational sectors exist on a world-scale. Organizations from different sectors interacting with each other in a particular terrain may acquire some common traits in their interaction which make them look more alike than they really are. Features of the terrain such as cultural symbols or languages make them look as if they belong together, but such a similarity is usually superficial. Struggles and interactions between organizations are among the most important driving forces of social change.

Now, interactions between organizations within and across sectors are different processes. Within sectors organizations interact with the same kind of power resources and compete for the same goals. In struggles between organizations from the same sector, it is fairly easy to see who is winning and who is losing and also what the gains and losses are. This is the case, for example, in warfare among nation-states, competition between companies or in political elections. Markets and politics are not separate social phenomena, though. They must be comprehended in terms of interaction between organizations.

Interaction across organizational sectors, on the other hand, is often confusing and unpredictable. Different kinds of power resources are set against each other and the organizations involved do not have the same goals. It is an interaction that is often contested and even considered illegitimate. When organizations from different sectors interact, they usually make demands on each other in order to prevent some of the operations of the other organization or to make it do things it would otherwise not do. This kind of interaction includes social phenomena such as corporatism, nepotism, taxation, customs, strikes, and social work.

Organizational interaction across sectors happens when the activities of different kinds of organization overlap in a certain place. The advantage of the particular power resources of the organizations involved is to a large extent determined by the terrain, and mobile organizations are sometimes able to choose the most suitable terrain for their interaction with other kinds of organizations.

The outcome of this kind of interaction is often inconclusive. There are rarely any obvious winners or losers. Rules are mostly unclear or non-existent. The interaction between organizations from different sectors is unorganized and unsettled. Mergers between organizations from different sectors are unlikely and when they occur they are highly controversial, such as the nationalization of capitalist enterprises.

In processes of interaction across sectors the result is often that one or both of the organizations have to change their practices and routines. It often means different forms of mutual adaptation, which can be rather complicated when several kinds of organization are involved.

Social change occurs through changing preconditions for interaction among the four organizational sectors. In particular parts of the social landscape, change means shifting combinations of organizations from different sectors. It is not a change of systems or structures; it is a change in organizational constellations. Organizations themselves acquire new technologies and forms of hierarchy and decisionmaking, which partly account for their ability to grow and expand. Still, their basic qualities remain remarkably constant. The births of new organizational types are rare historical events. The four organizational sectors: capitalist enterprises, nation-states, voluntary associations and families have been predominant for the last two hundred years, at least. The socialist regimes in Eastern Europe, for instance, were only an extreme form of nation-state. Organizations have increased in size and number and the combinations of various kinds of organization have changed dramatically, however. Should one so wish, it is of course possible to give names to some more stable constellations such as market economy, capitalism or socialism. But then these names or labels are almost as artificial as the names of the constellations in the sky. The only relevant conception of society today is world society. Nobody has proposed a label for this society, however.

In general, it seems as if the particular advantages of the power resources at the disposal of nation-states are becoming less effective and appropriate for the kinds of operation they are involved in. The value of the monopoly of violence is becoming less powerful in encounters with other kinds of organization with power resources better adjusted to the particular terrain where the interaction takes place. Moreover, the confinement of the monopoly of violence to one territory makes the power resources of nation-states inappropriate in interaction with supranational corporations or for solving problems of a global nature, such as threats against the environment.

The implication of an organizational theory of society is that social processes and social change must first of all be comprehended in their organizational settings and as the effects of interaction among organizations in various constellations. The relations between individuals and society can best be understood in terms of forms of organizational affiliation – membership, ownership, citizenship, kinship and employment – or in terms of asymmetric relations between the agents of corporate actors and single individuals in the semi-organized field.

Everyday life takes place in the realms of organizations. It does not occupy a sphere of its own. The relations between individuals and society can only be comprehended as the particular links between individuals and the organizations that are included in their domain of the social landscape. The preconditions for communicative action vary with organizational sector and with the organizational constellation. One cannot communicate with a system.

Concepts like power, democracy, social order, are meaningless and lose their content outside particular organizational settings. Processes such as rationalization, modernization, bureaucratization, specialization, professionalization, must be theorized and investigated in organizational terms. Social change is a process of organizational interaction, but the changes occur within organizations or in the semi-organized field.

Although organizations dominate social life global society is not organized. It is a mixture of organizations interacting in ever new constellations to increase their command over each other and over individuals in their environment. There is no higher order above or beyond these organizations, however. There is only disorder.

References

Ahrne, Göran (1989) *Byråkratin och statens inre gränser*. Stockholm: Raben och Sjögren.

Alexander, Jeffrey (1987) *Twenty Lectures: Sociological Theory since World War II*. New York: Columbia University Press.

Alexander, Jeffrey (1988a) 'Sociological theory today', in Neil Smelser (ed.), *Handbook of Sociology*. Beverly Hills, CA: Sage.

Alexander, Jeffrey (1988b) *Action and its Environments*. New York: Columbia University Press.

Alexander, Jeffrey, Giesen, Bernhard, Münch, Richard, and Smelser, Neil, J. (eds) (1987) *The Micro–Macro Link*. Berkeley: University of California Press.

Alexander, Jeffrey and Giesen, Bernhard (1988) 'From reduction to linkage: the long view of the micro–macro debate' in Jeffrey Alexander, *Action and its Environments*. New York: Columbia University Press.

Barbalet, J. M. (1988) *Citizenship: Rights, Struggle and Class Inequality*. Milton Keynes: Open University Books.

Barkman, Clas (1989) 'Electroluxkulturen nyckeln till framgång', *Dagens Nyheter*, July/August.

Berger, Peter and Luckmann, Thomas (1967) *The Social Construction of Reality*. New York: Anchor Books.

Braudel, Fernand (1982) *The Wheels of Commerce*. London: William Collins.

Burawoy, Michael (1985) *The Politics of Production*. London: Verso.

Burrell, Gibson and Morgan, Gareth (1979) *Sociological Paradigms and Organizational Analysis*. Aldershot: Gower.

Cawson, Alan (ed.) (1985) *Organized Interests and the State*. London: Sage.

Cohen, Michael D., March, James G. and Olsen, Johan P. (1982)

'People, problems, solutions and the ambiguity of relevance' in James G. March and Johan P. Olsen (eds), *Ambiguity and Choice in Organizations*. Bergen: Universitetsforlaget.

Coleman, James, S. (1982) *The Asymmetric Society*. Syracuse: Syracuse University Press.

Collins, Randall (1986) *Weberian Sociological Theory*. Cambridge: Cambridge University Press.

Collins, Randall (1988) 'The micro contribution to macro sociology', *Sociological Theory*, 6 (2): 242–53.

Crozier, Michel (1964) *The Bureaucratic Phenomenon*. Chicago: University of Chicago Press.

Cyert, Richard M. and March, James G. (1963) *A Behavioral Theory of the Firm*. Englewood Cliffs, NJ: Prentice-Hall.

DiMaggio, Paul J. and Powell, Walter W. (1983) 'The iron cage revisited: institutional isomorphism and collective rationality in organizational fields', *American Sociological Review*, 48 (April): 147–60.

Donaldson, Lex (1985) *In Defence of Organization Theory: a Reply to the Critics*. Cambridge: Cambridge University Press.

Elvander, Nils (1989) 'The double challenge to the trade unions: alternative forms of remuneration and internationalization' in *Sociology in the World: Essays in Honour of Ulf Himmelstrand*. Uppsala: Department of Sociology.

Etzioni, Amitai (1961) *A Comparative Analysis of Complex Organizations*. New York: Free Press of Glencoe.

Etzioni, Amitai (1988) *The Moral Dimension: Toward a New Economics*. New York: Free Press.

Foucault, Michel (1979) *Discipline and Punish: the Birth of the Prison*. Harmondsworth: Penguin.

Gerth, Hans and Mills, C. Wright (1970) *Character and Social Structure: the Psychology of Social Institutions*. London: Routledge and Kegan Paul.

Giddens, Anthony (1979) *Central Problems in Social Theory*. London: Hutchinson.

Giddens, Anthony (1984) *The Constitution of Society*. Cambridge: Polity Press.

Goffman, Erving (1972) *Relations in Public: Microstudies of the Public Order*. New York: Harper and Row.

Habermas, Jürgen (1984) *The Theory of Communicative Action: Volume One*. Boston: Beacon Press.

Habermas, Jürgen (1985) *Der philosophische Diskurs der Moderne*. Frankfurt am Main: Suhrkamp Verlag.

Habermas, Jürgen (1987) *The Theory of Communicative Action: Volume Two*. Boston: Beacon Press.

Himmelstrand, Ulf, Ahrne, Göran, Lundberg, Leif and Lundberg, Lars (1981) *Beyond Welfare Capitalism*. London: Heinemann.

Hirschman, Albert (1970) *Exit, Voice and Loyalty: Responses to Decline in Firms, Organizations, and States*. Cambridge, MA: Harvard University Press.

Hirschman, Albert (1981) *Essays in Trespassing: Economics to Politics and Beyond*. Cambridge: Cambridge University Press.

Hirschman, Albert (1982) *Shifting Involvements: Private Interest and Public Action*. Oxford: Basil Blackwell.

Knorr-Cetina, K. and Cicourel, A.V. (eds) (1981) *Advances in Social Theory and Methodology: Toward an Integration of Micro- and Macro-Sociologies*. Boston: Routledge and Kegan Paul.

Korpi, Walter (1985) 'Power resources approach vs. action and conflict: on causal and intentional explanations in the study of power', *Sociological Theory*, 3 (2): 31–45.

Laing, R. D. and Cooper, D. G. (1964) *Reason and Violence: a Decade of Sartre's Philosophy 1950–1960*. London: Tavistock Publications.

Laumann, Edward O. and Knoke, David (1987) *The Organizational State: Social Choice in National Policy Domains*. Madison: The University of Wisconsin Press.

Lindblom, Charles (1971) *Politics and Markets*. New York: Basic Books.

Lipsky, Michael (1980) *Street-Level Bureaucracy*. New York: Russell Sage Foundation.

Littler, Craig (1982) *The Development of the Labour Process in Capitalist Societies*. London: Heinemann Educational Books.

Lundberg, Lars (1982) *Från lag till arbetsmiljö*. Stockholm: Liber.

Mann, Michael (1986) *The Sources of Social Power: Volume 1*. Cambridge: Cambridge University Press.

March, James G. and Simon, Herbert A. (1958) *Organizations*. New York: John Wiley.

Marshall, Thomas H. (1965) *Class, Citizenship and Social Development*. New York: Anchor Books.

Massey, Doreen (1984) 'Introduction: geography matters' in Doreen Massey and John Allen (eds), *Geography Matters: a Reader*. Cambridge: Cambridge University Press.

Merton, Robert (1968) 'Bureaucratic structure and personality' in Robert Merton, *Social Theory and Social Structure*. 1968 enlarged edition. New York: Free Press.

Meyer, John W. and Rowan, Brian (1977) 'Institutionalized

organizations: formal structure as myth and ceremony', *American Journal of Sociology*, 83(2): 340–63.

Meyer, John W., Boli, John and Thomas, George M. (1987) 'Ontology and rationalization in the western cultural account' in George M. Thomas, John W. Meyer, Fransisco O. Ramirez and John Boli (eds), *Institutional Structure: Constituting State, Society and the Individual*. Newbury Park, CA: Sage.

Meyer, Marshall W. (1985), *Limits to Bureaucratic Growth*. Berlin: Walter de Gruyter.

Meyer, Marshall W. (1987), 'The growth of public and private bureaucracies', *Theory and Society*, 16 (2): 215–35.

Mills, C. Wright (1970) *The Sociological Imagination*. Harmondsworth: Penguin.

Mintzberg, Henry (1979) *The Structuring of Organizations*. Englewood Cliffs, NJ: Prentice-Hall.

Offe, Claus (1984) *Contradictions of the Welfare State*. Edited by John Keane. London: Hutchinson.

Perrow, Charles (1967) 'A framework for the comparative analysis of organizations', *American Sociological Review*, 32 (2): 194–208.

Perrow, Charles (1984) *Normal Accidents: Living with High-Risk Technologies*. New York: Basic Books.

Perrow, Charles (1986) *Complex Organizations: a Critical Essay*. Third edition. New York: Random House.

Pfeffer, Jeffrey and Salancik, Gerald R. (1978) *The External Control of Organizations*. New York: Harper and Row.

Poulantzas, Nicos (1978) *State, Power, Socialism*. London: Verso.

Rothstein, Bo (1986) *Den socialdemokratiska staten*. Lund: Arkiv.

Rothstein, Bo (1987) 'Corporatism and reformism: the social democratic institutionalization of class conflict', *Acta Sociologica*, 30 (3/4): 295–312.

Rusbult, Caryl, Farrell, Dan, Rogers, Glen, and Mainous Arch III (1988) 'Impact of exchange variables on exit, voice, loyalty, and neglect: an integrative model of responses to declining job satisfactions', *Academy of Management Journal*, 31 (3): 599–627.

Sack, Robert David (1986) *Human Territoriality: its Theory and History*. Cambridge: Cambridge University Press.

Sartre, Jean-Paul (1968) *Search for a Method*. New York: Vintage Books.

Sartre, Jean-Paul (1976) *Critique of Dialectical Reason I: Theory of Practical Ensembles*. London: New Left Books.

Schutz, Alfred (1962) 'On multiple realities', in Alfred Schutz,

Collected Papers I: the Problem of Social Reality. Edited by Maurice Natanson. The Hague: Martinus Nijhoff.

Scott, Richard W. (1987) *Organizations: Rational, Natural and Open Systems*. Second edition. Englewood Cliffs, NJ: Prentice-Hall.

Scott, Richard, W. and Meyer, John W. (1983) 'The organization of societal sectors' in John W. Meyer and Richard W. Scott, *Organizational Environments: Ritual and Rationality*. Beverly Hills, CA: Sage.

Skocpol, Theda (1984) 'Emerging agendas and recurrent strategies in historical sociology' in Theda Skocpol (ed.), *Vision and Method in Historical Sociology*. Cambridge: Cambridge University Press.

Soja, Edward, W. (1985) 'The spatiality of social life: towards a transformative retheorisation', in Derek Gregory and John Urry (eds), *Social Relations and Spatial Structures*. London: Macmillan.

Stryjan, Yohanan (1989) *Impossible Organizations. On Self-management and Organizational Reproduction*. New York: Greenwood Press.

Thompson, James (1967) *Organizations in Action*. New York: McGraw-Hill.

Tilly, Charles (1984) *Big Structures, Large Processes, Huge Comparisons*. New York: Russell Sage Foundation.

Wallerstein, Immanuel (1986) 'Societal development, or development of the world-system?' *International Sociology* 1 (1): 3–17.

Weber, Max (1968) *Economy and Society: Volumes One and Two*. Edited by Guenther Roth and Claus Wittich. Berkeley: University of California Press.

Weick, Karl E. (1976) 'Educational organizations as loosely coupled systems', *Administrative Science Quarterly*, 21 (March): 1–19.

Williamson, Oliver (1975) *Markets and Hierarchy: Analysis and Antitrust Implications*. New York: Free Press.

Williamson, Oliver (1981) 'The Economics of Organization: the Transaction Cost Approach', *American Journal of Sociology*, 87 (3): 548–77.

Woodward, Joan (1965) *Industrial Organization: Theory and Practice*. London: Oxford University Press.

Wright, Erik Olin and Kwang-Yeong Shin (1988) 'Temporality and class analysis: a comparative study of the effects of class trajectory and class structure on class consciousness in Sweden and the United States', *Sociological Theory*, 6 (Spring): 58–84.

Zey-Ferrell, Mary and Aiken, Michael (eds) (1981) *Complex Organizations: Critical Perspectives*. Glenview, IL: Scott, Foresman.

Index